The Power of the Media Specialist to Improve Academic Achievement and Strengthen At-Risk Students

Jami Biles Jones, Ph.D
Alana M. Zambone, Ph.D

Linworth
Books

Professional Development Resources for K–12
Library Media and Technology Specialists

Library of Congress Cataloging-in-Publication Data

Jones, Jami Biles.
  The power of media specialists to raise academic achievement and strengthen at-risk students / Jami Biles Jones, Alana M. Zambone.
      p. cm.
  Includes bibliographical references and index.
  ISBN 1-58683-229-8 (pbk.)
  1. Instructional materials personnel–United States. 2. School libraries–United States. 3. Academic achievement–United States. 4. Children with social disabilities–Education–United States. I. Zambone, Alana M. II. Title.
  Z675.S3J7274 2008
  027.8--dc22
                        2007030116

Cynthia Anderson: Editor
Carol Simpson: Editorial Director
Judi Repman: Consulting Editor

Published by Linworth Publishing, Inc.
3650 Olentangy River Road, Suite 250
Columbus, Ohio 43214

Trademarks: Rather than put a trademark symbol with every occurrence of a trademarked name, we note that we are using the names simply in an editorial fashion and to the benefit of the trademark owner, with no intention of infringement of the trademark.

All URL addresses are current as of publication date. If the reader encounters a broken link, please search the Web for the topic and you will find a similar working link.

5 4 3 2

This book is dedicated to the students who have been left behind by the American educational system and the mentors who intercede on their behalf.

Table of Contents

Table of Figures

Introduction

American education is failing many students, but especially students of color, from low-income families, with disabilities, or those who have limited English proficiency. These students are the focus of *No Child Left Behind* (NCLB), the 2001 revision of the *Elementary and Secondary Education Act* which was signed into law on January 8, 2002. As much as educators complain about NCLB it is difficult to argue against its purpose that all students will succeed regardless of race, ethnicity, family income, dominant language, or handicap. NCLB is the continuation of 1963 civil rights legislation whose unmistakable goal is to ensure that students who have previously been left out, pushed to the side, and received inadequate schooling will no longer be ignored (Thernstrom et al. 3). The message to educators is they must find ways to reach all students.

The purpose of *The Power of the Media Specialist to Improve Academic Achievement and Strengthen At-Risk Students* is to position media specialists to become instructional change agents. This is done in three ways. First, the book presents to media specialists the findings of research that shows the best ways to increase academic achievement and strengthen at-risk youth. Second, it provides media specialists with the knowledge and strategies based on research-based practices to change the culture of the school library program, and consequently the school. Third, it is a blueprint for school library programs to become the *heart* of the school and integral to student achievement.

Readers will be introduced to two concepts throughout this book. The first concept is dispositions, which are defined as personal, professional, and ethical qualities. These dispositions are instrumental to improving academic achievement and strengthening at-risk youth by creating an environment in which students flourish. The second concept is systems change, which is a process that is necessary if the media specialist desires to build a school library program that significantly impacts student achievement. To do this, the media specialist must first understand the complexity of the educational failure problem and who is most at risk. Second, the media specialist must understand the body of research that clarifies the strategies and practices that improve academic achievement and strengthen at-risk youth and those that are less effective. Third, the media specialist will reflect on the previous steps as well as analyze and synthesize the research findings so as to develop a vision of a school library program that supports student achievement. Fourth, media specialists will seek out other faculty, staff, and administrators with similar visions and together they will develop a shared vision for creating a school library program that significantly contributes to school-wide achievement. Fifth, the media specialist will work to bring life to this shared vision.

The Power of the Media Specialist to Improve Academic Achievement and Strengthen At-Risk Students is suggested reading for university faculty who are preparing media specialists to work in schools where there is increasing pressure to make a difference and improve academic achievement. Library science and school media coursework must be infused with knowledge of effective strategies, such as the importance of supporting reading by building students' background knowledge, collaboration, and how dispositions of the media specialist can boost the power of the school library program because no one strategy works well with all students. The *one size fits all* paradigm of the past is a fallacy and always was. Rather, media specialists who want to make a difference use a variety of techniques, strategies, and dispositions. School district media supervisors can use *The Power of the Media Specialist to Improve Academic Achievement and Strengthen At-Risk Students* to provide leadership and vision while helping media specialists develop these dispositions, and to focus the efforts of media specialists on increasing student achievement. Sections titled *Think About…* and *Can Do…* scattered throughout the book can be used as discussion starters.

Library science professionals have conducted numerous studies to measure the positive impact that a qualified media specialist and a strong school library program has on a school's test scores. Since the 1990s, Lance and his colleagues, Todd and Kuhlthau, Baumbach, Callison, Baughman, and others have shown the impact that school libraries have on student achievement. These research efforts have identified specific factors such as a professional and certified media specialist, strong collection of books and other resources, flexible scheduling, increased amount of time the school library is available to students, collaboration, and technology integrated into the learning/teaching process.

Many practices, strategies, and dispositions described in this book may seem simplistic but actually pack a big punch. In the book *The Tipping Point: How Little Things Can Make a Big Difference,* author Malcolm Gladwell describes how the theory of "Broken Windows" can turn around negative situations. Epidemics, which he defines as negative situations affecting a large number of persons [author's note: low test scores and significant gaps in achievement fit this description], "can be reversed, can be tipped, by tinkering with the smallest details of the immediate environment" (146). He describes how in the 1980s one small change turned around the impending collapse of the New York City subway which was overwhelmed by crime, filth, and trains that did not run on schedule. At the urging of a consultant, the New York Transit Authority focused on eliminating graffiti. Singling out this problem may seem inconsequential compared to other challenges facing the subway system, but it was viewed as the "symbolic collapse of the system" (142). Eradicating graffiti was the tipping point—the small change—that transformed a beleaguered subway system into one of the world's best. After reading *The Power of the Media Specialist to Improve Academic Achievement and Strengthen At-Risk Students*, media specialists will likewise recognize the importance of implementing the small changes—the tipping points—that can transform low-achieving media programs into high-achieving ones.

The Power of the Media Specialist to Improve Academic Achievement and Strengthen At-Risk Students is organized into three sections. The first section provides the foundation for understanding the problem of academic failure and at-risk youth. Chapter One describes the current state of education for students who are not successful in school. Chapter Two explores the characteristics and conditions that contribute to or impede students' success. Chapter Three describes the laws that have been enacted to ensure that all students have equal access to education.

The second section describes effective strategies from research in librarianship, education, and the social sciences that improve students' academic achievement. Chapter Four describes the findings of the impact studies designed by Lance and his colleagues and replicated in at least 16 states, as well as others that indicate that effective school libraries do improve academic achievement. Chapter Five explores successful frameworks, approaches, and strategies for improving academic achievement and strengthening youth such as resiliency, research identified by Robert J. Marzano, and the National Dropout Prevention Center/Network at Clemson University in South Carolina.

In the third section, the strategies, techniques, and information from the first two sections will be applied specifically to the school library to expand the media specialist's arsenal for closing the achievement gap and strengthening at-risk students. Chapter Six provides strategies and techniques for raising academic achievement and strengthening youth. Chapter Seven provides readers with information about systems change for the purpose of developing an environment that benefits students and evaluating whether the program has been successful.

Media specialists, university faculty, and district media supervisors who read this book with an open mind will view academic failure in a different light. The evidence is too strong to ignore the impact that small changes—tipping points like graffiti in a subway—have on closing the achievement gap and strengthening at-risk students.

SECTION ONE

The Significance of the Problem

Introduction

The numbers are astounding and they point one way: to failure. As you read this section, do so with empathy by putting yourself in the shoes of students who may have limited resources, few options, and attend an underperforming school. These students did not ask to receive an inferior education or immigrate to America or be born into a low-socioeconomic status (SES) family, but most are coping as well as they can.

"A journey of a thousand miles must begin with a single step," wrote Lao-Tzu, the father of Taoism, in the sixth century B.C. The first step in our journey is to understand the dynamics of educational failure, the populations most at risk, and the legislation that has been enacted to protect at-risk students. This understanding provides the foundation for looking at the problem in a new light and beginning to develop a vision for creating a school library program that addresses the academic needs of students.

There is a term in the resiliency literature that is used to describe a special individual who is able to help youth develop the competencies to move from at-risk to resilient. The term is turnaround and "these turnaround teachers and mentors are described as building, in their own personal styles and ways, three crucial environmental protective factors: connection, competence, and contribution" (Benard). The turnaround media specialist is proactive and a divergent, out-of-the-box thinker who is able to analyze, synthesize, and apply research findings to create a school library program that benefits students. The turnaround media specialist cares about students and connects with them. He reflects this by building a library program that meets the unique needs of students in the school and community.

As you read the chapters in this section, apply what you are learning to your own situation. Reflect on the following questions: Does the school where you teach prepare students for academic success? If not, what factors impede student progress? Who is at risk of failing and how many students does this represent? What is the school doing to improve the academic achievement of at-risk students? How is legislation such as *No Child Left Behind* and *Individuals with Disabilities Education Act* applied in your school? How is the media specialist incorporating this legislation into the school's library program to meet the needs of at-risk students?

CHAPTER ONE

How Significant is the Achievement Gap?

Imagine at the end of every school day that 181 students climb onto buses never to return. Or imagine the chaos if one-third of all airplanes that take off from American airports crashed instead of landing at their destinations (Schargel). The reality is **one-third of American students** do not graduate from high school.

Although dropping out of school before earning a high school diploma is not a new occurrence (in the 1940s fewer than half the individuals ages 25-29 graduated), the recent focus on improving graduation rates and reducing dropout rates is a result of the *No Child Left Behind* (NCLB) legislation which requires that states collect statistics to document how well its students are meeting educational standards. Even before NCLB was signed into law in January 2002, earlier reports such as the 1983 *A Nation At Risk* and *National Goals 2000* addressed the dropout problem.

The failure of students to complete high school is a travesty on many levels. First, the high dropout rate is the clearest indicator that the American educational system is not working for many students. The high school diploma is the credential that measures whether or not the educational system is functioning as intended. Second, the diploma acts as a gatekeeper: students who have it are on track to a brighter future with more options; those without it will likely experience economic struggles. In large measure, this piece of paper determines a graduate's future profession, as well as the house and car he can afford. Third, as the American workplace becomes increasingly high tech and requires employees to be critical thinkers, it is imperative that youth have access to education that promotes these skills and abilities; however, many students do not.

It used to be that students without a diploma who were willing to work hard could find good-paying jobs in factories, but many of these opportunities have either dried up or gone overseas. Americans today are not only competing against neighbors for scarce jobs, but also well-educated and eager graduates of well-performing school systems in countries like India and China. Fourth, the economic loss to the individual and society because of chronic underemployment and dependence on jobs that pay minimum wage is significant. As a society it behooves adults to ensure that youth are able to participate economically, politically, socially, and culturally. The key to this participation is education.

What do we know about students who drop out? When students drop out—and many begin to consider this an option before 13 years of age—it is an expense that the citizens of this nation must shoulder for the rest of the dropout's life. Some of these expenses can be quantified. The Alliance for Excellent Education estimates that the almost 1.3 million students who didn't graduate from U.S. high schools in 2004 will cost the nation more than $325 billion in lost wages, taxes, and productivity over their lifetime. "This is a very conservative estimate," said Alliance president and former governor of West Virginia, Bob Wise. "There's so much that it doesn't include—like the much higher earnings that would be realized if some of the kids not only got their high school diploma but also went on to college" (Riggs et al). Other estimates are as high as $944 billion in lost revenues and $24 billion in welfare and crime-related spending.

High school graduation and drop out is very complex to understand for several reasons. First, there is no single definition of high school completion. In section 1111(b)(2)(C)(vi) of the NCLB legislation, it is defined as the "percentage of students who graduate from a secondary school with a regular diploma in a standard number of years." In contrast, the National Center for Education Statistics (NCES), the branch of the U.S. Department of Education responsible for collecting and analyzing data that are related to education in the United States, uses a broader definition that includes all diplomas and certificates of completion or other formal indications of high school completion.

The second reason it is difficult to grasp the complexity of high school graduation and drop out is that the rates are computed differently by states, the Federal government, and organizations—each paints a slightly different picture. For instance, even though the NCES required states to submit high school graduation rates disaggregated by race/ethnicity, disability status, low-income status, English language proficiency, gender, and migrant status, but this did not always occur. For 2004-2004, seven states did not disaggregate the data at all and many more reported either full or partial data. North Carolina claimed its graduation rate was 97% by calculating not the "percentage of students who entered in the ninth grade and received a diploma four years later, but on the percentage of graduates who get their diplomas in four years or less" (Hall 6).

The third reason it is difficult to grasp the complexity is that when data is disaggregated, graduation rates can vary widely by race and ethnicity. Even though the high school graduation rate is estimated by the Urban Institute to be 68% and by the NCES to be 86.5%, the problem is much worse for certain groups of students because "tremendous racial gaps exist. Students from historically disadvantaged minority groups (American Indian, Latino, African American) have little more than a fifty-fifty chance of finishing high school with a diploma. By comparison, graduation rates for whites and Asians are seventy-five and seventy-seven percent nationally" (Swanson v).

Although graduation statistics are readily available for high schools and school districts, there are different ways to calculate these figures. One way is the NCLB formula described above. A second way is to apply the Cumulative Promotion Index (CPI) created by Christopher Swanson of the Urban Institute. Using enrollment and diploma-count data from the NCES, the CPI is based on "the probability that a student entering ninth grade will complete high school on time with a regular diploma" (Swanson). To calculate the CPI, the number of tenth graders in one year is compared to the number of ninth graders in the previous year to determine the percentage of ninth graders who were promoted. This is calculated for the other grades (eleventh to tenth, twelfth to eleventh, and graduates to twelfth). These four ratios are multiplied to arrive at an estimated graduation rate. Using the CPI method, the U.S. graduation rate for all students in 2001 was 68% (Hall).

A third way to calculate graduation rates is to apply the Promoting Power Index (PPI), which is an estimate of how well schools retain students until twelfth grade. This formula was developed by Robert Balfanz and Nettie Legters of Johns Hopkins University. The PPI compares the number of twelfth graders enrolled in a high school to the number of ninth graders (or tenth graders in a high school consisting of grades ten through twelve). A school with 1,000 students in ninth grade and 800 students in twelfth grade has a PPI of 80%. This formula loses some of its reliability when there are drastic shifts in population that affect the school. However, Balfanz and Letgers argue that the PPI can be used as a graduation-rate estimate based on the assumption that "high schools in which the number of seniors closely approximates the number of freshman four years earlier will have high graduation rates...because most students will have remained in school, been promoted in a timely fashion, and are on course to graduate" (Balfanz and Legters 3). According to these researchers more than 2,000 high schools—fully 18 percent of all high schools—have a PPI of less than 60%. These low-PPI schools serve a disproportionate number of students of color and low SES.

Can Do...

Visit <www.standup.org> to learn how your state and local community's test scores and graduation rates compare to others.

Graduation May Not Be Enough

In April 2006, Oprah Winfrey presented a two-day *Oprah* special, "America's Silent Epidemic." She said, "I'm blown away that this isn't on every parent's mind." The "this" that Winfrey refers to is the millions of students who are dropping out, falling through the cracks, and not receiving an education that allows them to thrive in college. She asked Bill Gates, the billionaire-founder of the Microsoft Corporation, who is committed to changing American education, "If the educational system were a business, how would you rate it?" His response: "It would be bankrupt" ("America's Silent Epidemic").

Winfrey arranged for students attending two very different high schools to trade places with each other for the purpose of highlighting the significant educational inequities that exist. Students at Harper High, a poor inner-city Chicago school, spent the day at Nequa Valley High School in the wealthy suburb of Naperville, Illinois, and vice versa. At Harper High, only 40% of students graduate; at Nequa Valley, 99%. Awestruck is the only way to describe the reaction of the Harper High students as they toured the modern Nequa Valley facility that includes an Olympic-size swimming pool and state-of-the-art gym. Nequa Valley boasts a Grammy-award-winning music program and 24 rigorous Advanced Placement courses to help students attain college credit. Harper High is Nequa Valley's polar opposite—it is old and rundown, the pool is moldy and does not hold water, the gym equipment is broken, the marching band has no instruments, and few Advanced Placement courses are offered. As the crow flies there is little physical distance between the schools, but the educational opportunities available to students could not be further apart.

Although students from both schools recognized the inequities, one Harper High student summed it up this way: "I've been cheated." Tiffany, a top student at Harper High who aspires to major in business administration in college, realized her dream was in jeopardy after attending the Nequa Valley trigonometry class. "I was looking at their math problems that they're doing and I was thinking, 'What language are they doing…I'll be lost when I get to college'" ("America's Silent Epidemic").

It is not just inner-city schools populated by students of color that are failing students. Beth Martin, a graduate of a high school in Hancock County, Tennessee, where almost 98% of the population is white and 37.5% of children under 18 live below the poverty line, almost flunked out of college even though she had taken the most challenging courses her high school offered, earned a perfect 4.0 grade point average, was class valedictorian, and served as president of the student council. Martin's problems began soon after entering college on scholarship when she realized that her high school had not prepared her for the rigors of the pre-medicine program. Only by working much harder than other students and teaching herself has she been able to stay in college; but this has set her back more than one year. Martin suspects that her dream of becoming a doctor may never materialize ("America's Silent Epidemic").

Students know and care that they are being denied quality education. Cushman interviewed 65 students to gather their perspectives on high school culture and climate. Sixty percent of the students interviewed were of color, and almost none came from privileged backgrounds. Students told her they want classes that are engaging. When "classes offer only a steady diet of tedium, these students would just as soon forget about school and look to the media, the streets, or peer relationships for interest and stimulation" (34). They asked for hands-on projects that combine high-interest topics with academic competencies, fair and consistent treatment, inspiring role models, and extracurricular activities such as sports and clubs that help them express their passions, feelings, and competence. The worst inequity occurs when students do not have access to rigorous classes that are well taught.

Think About...

- How can you teach information literacy skills using topics of high interest to students?
- How can you be a role model?
- How can you encourage student interest in sports and hobbies?

High School Graduation and College Readiness Are Not the Same

Tiffany and Beth stand as examples to illustrate that even when students graduate from high school with good grades, preparation for college-level academics is not guaranteed. The two problems being discussed in this chapter—high school dropout and college readiness—are related and can be visualized as an iceberg. The tip of the iceberg is the high school dropout problem. What lies beneath the water line is not so easily seen—it is the problem of college readiness, which is integral to any discussion about high school graduation. The root cause of both problems is systemic failure of an educational system to adopt strategies that prevent dropout and encourage all students to achieve.

Using Department of Education data for the class of 2000-2001, Greene and Forster of the Manhattan Institute, an influential think tank that disseminates new ideas about hot-topic issues, were able to estimate the percentage of students who graduate high school as well as the percentage of students who graduate from high school ready to attend a four-year college. Their findings indicate that:

- Although 70% of all students in public high schools graduated in 2001, only 32% exited high school qualified to attend four-year colleges
- Although slightly more than 50% of all African-American and Latino students graduated that year, only 20% and 16% respectively were college-ready

- Although the graduation rate for Caucasian students was 72%; for Asians, 79%; and for American Indians, 54%, their college readiness rates were much lower at 37%, 38%, and 14% (Greene and Forster).

ACT, the nonprofit organization responsible for the college entrance exam bearing the same name, is a leader in researching college readiness shortcomings. Its policy report, *College Readiness Begins in Middle School*, found that among students who aspired to attend a two- or four-year college, only two-thirds described their high school program of study as college preparatory (Wimberly and Noeth).

A coalition of organizations such as the Bill & Melinda Gates Foundation, the Broad Foundation, MTV, and the Public Interest formed to address a common goal: demanding a solution to our education crisis. At <www.standup.org> rates for high school graduation, college readiness, college enrollment, and the percentage of students who complete college within six years are available. The results of state tests as well as the National Assessment of Educational Progress, called *The Nation's Report Card,* are also available.

American education is a complex system that by most accounts is failing between one-half and one-third of students. Many of these students belong to the four categories of students targeted by NCLB who have traditionally not had access to quality education. Quality education is a civil rights issue. In the book *Shame of the Nation: The Restoration of Apartheid Schooling in America*, Jonathan Kozol states that "conditions have grown worse for inner-city children in the 15 years since federal courts began dismantling the landmark ruling in *Brown v. Board of Education*" (front flap). Inner-city students are more likely than other students to attend low-PPI schools and less likely to graduate from high school. In the next chapter you will be presented with specific information about students who are most at risk of educational failure.

Resources to Learn More about This Topic

The National Dropout Prevention Center/Network at <www.dropoutprevention. org> has many resources to learn about and solve this problem.

The Urban Institute at <www.urban.org> is a nonpartisan policy group that researches timely topics such as education, crime, and taxes. Available reports include *Counting High School Graduates when Graduates Count: Measuring Graduation Rates under the High Stakes of NCLB* and *Losing Our Future: How Minority Youth are Being Left Behind.*

The Bill & Melinda Gates Foundation at <www.gatesfoundation.org> seeks to ensure that all students in the United States graduate from high school ready for college, work, and citizenship. Available reports include *High Schools for the New Millennium: Imagine the Possibilities* and *Silent Epidemic: Perspectives on High School Dropouts.*

CHAPTER TWO

Who is At Risk of Failing?

Each year, approximately one-third of all high school students drop out rather than graduate. As shown in Chapter One, the conditions leading to students being at risk for school failure are complex and multifaceted. When researchers and school personnel predict who might be at risk for failure, they generally consider only one of two factors. The first is individual characteristics such as race or ethnicity, low socioeconomic status (SES), family structure, or disability. The second is school practices such as inflexible schedules, narrow curricula, rigid instruction, tracking, and low expectations. More recently, educators have begun to believe that in order to identify who might be at risk and improve their academic achievement, it is necessary to examine both the student's circumstances, and the school's environment.

> ### Think About...
> Visit your school district's Web site to learn how many students are receiving free or reduced lunch, are members of minority groups, or are second language learners.

Two assumptions of education personnel negatively influence most efforts to meet the needs of at-risk students. The first is that achievement is primarily the responsibility of the individual, not the school. The second is that schools can only do so much to keep students of color and low SES from failing. Yet, research shows that the schools which are helping at-risk students to be successful operate on the premise that when a school responds to the culture of the students and community it serves, it will adopt educational approaches and interventions that build resiliency and ensure success for vulnerable populations (Astuto et al.).

Blaming dropout solely on students, families, or schools does little to solve the at-risk problem. School reformers who seek to understand at-risk students often employ an ecological systems perspective, which means that they take into account the environments and circumstances of students and schools separately and in relation to each other. An ecological systems perspective recognizes that neither students nor schools develop in isolation or function in a vacuum.

Within this perspective, school personnel appreciate the importance of building connections between students' homes, their neighborhoods, and the school. Often schools, students, and families are stressed by conditions outside their control that impact student achievement, such as socioeconomic status, race and ethnicity, immigration, limited English proficiency, and special education placement.

Think About...

Can you think of a stressor you experienced outside of school and how it affected you while at work? Did anyone offer to help or listen? How did their support affect the way you approached your job?

Identify one factor beyond your control that makes your job more difficult, for example, limited funding or red-tape in getting new materials or equipment. How does this make you feel about your work sometimes?

Socioeconomic Status

The most significant predictor that a student will drop out of high school is low-socioeconomic status (SES). A family's socioeconomic status is based on family income, parental education level, parental occupation, and social status in the community such as contacts within the community, group associations, and the community's perception of the family. Families with low SES lack the financial, social, and educational support that higher-SES families enjoy. Low-SES families may have inadequate or limited access to community resources that promote and support children's development and school readiness.

When Almeida et al. analyzed the NELS data which tracked the educational progress of approximately 25,000 eighth graders from 1988 to 2000, they found that "socioeconomic status, rather than race, is the key indicator for dropping out" and that dropping out is a "full-fledged epidemic in central cities and other low-income communities" (iii). Many low-SES students are clustered in the urban or rural schools that are more likely to have a low Cumulative Promotion Index or Promoting Power Index as discussed in Chapter One. Jonathan Kozol, author of the book *The Shame of the Nation,* likens this to the restoration of apartheid schooling in America.

Poverty is the distinguishing characteristic of low SES. Although Caucasian and Asian students do experience poverty, the rate is double for Latino, African American, and Native American children. For more information about who is poor in this country visit <www.census.gov/hhes/www/poverty/poverty.html>.

A must-read for media specialists is the work of Ruby Payne, a career educator who writes extensively about the mindset of economic classes. Her work is especially influential at this time because the number of low-SES and poor children is increasing and educational systems are struggling to meet these children's needs. Payne contends that educators often view the world from a middle-class perspective and may not understand the values of low-SES students. Likewise, low-SES students may not relate to middle-class values that emphasize achievement at the expense of relationships. As a result, poor students may have a difficult time functioning in the classroom.

Payne characterizes poverty as the "extent to which an individual does without resources" (22) such as money; the ability to control one's emotions; the acquired skills of reading, writing, and math; believing in a divine purpose; being physically healthy; having a support system in time of need; nurturing role models who are not self-destructive, and knowledge of hidden rules. She identifies and defines two kinds of poverty, generational and situational. Generational poverty is defined as being in poverty for two generations or longer. Situational poverty does not span generations but is caused by unplanned circumstances such as death, illness, or divorce.

According to Payne, the following characteristics that are likely to be present in generational poverty can impact a child's education:

- Students may have a difficult time studying at home because of significant background noise from television and participatory conversations in which one or more people are talking at the same time
- Students may have a difficult time committing their thoughts to paper because oral-language and storytelling is valued more than writing
- Students may experience difficulty thinking in abstract terms and theories because life is about survival and practical considerations; for instance, jobs are about making enough money to survive, not career satisfaction
- Students may not understand that discipline should result in change because in generational poverty its purpose is penance and forgiveness
- Students may not understand that they have options to be examined because in generational poverty thinking tends to be polarized
- Students may not think about the future because what counts is today; goal setting and planning are not part of generational poverty
- Students value and respond to a sense of humor
- Students may need to be taught organization skills

Payne's message to educators is they must understand the culture of their students if their teaching is to be effective. While organization skills, future orientation, abstract thinking, and goal setting may not be a priority in generational poverty, a sense of humor, an emphasis on personality, and an oral tradition are strengths to be taught to and respected. Teachers must transcend their value system and understand their students' if they are to be effective educators. While anecdotal evidence and research indicates that differences in SES are at the heart of the achievement gap, other studies suggest that these differences play a minor role (Phillips et. al.). These studies reinforce the need to look beyond student characteristics to school environments and personnel to identify unequal treatments that may account for academic differences by class, race, and ethnicity.

Think About...

Do you know how much poverty there is in your community and state? To find this information visit:

- The U.S. Department of Education's School District Demographics at <nces.ed.gov/surveys/sdss/index.asp>
- The U.S. Census Bureau at <censtats.census.gov> or <www.fedstats.gov> (provides statistics on population projections as well as other counts that impact education)

Race and Ethnicity

According to a 2006 press release by the U.S. Census Bureau, persons of color account for 33 percent of our population. The largest and fastest growing group is Latinos, with African Americans making up the second largest group. Interestingly, Latinos make up almost half of the population increase between 2004 and 2005. Another interesting characteristic of the Latino population is that their average age is nearly ten years younger than the average age of the overall population in the U.S. because they include a higher percentage of youth under the age of 18 than any other group.

Students who are members of ethnic minorities in this country, particularly Latinos and African Americans, enter school facing conditions that put them at risk for failure. A look back over our nation's history reveals that at one time or another all of the following groups of non-Caucasian citizens—Native Americans, African Americans, Latinos, and Asians—were systematically excluded and segregated and their opportunities were limited (Spring). This history influences today's beliefs and assumptions about each group. Schools, as part of the culture, reflect these beliefs and assumptions; however, school personnel may not be aware of their effects on expectations and opportunities provided students of color and poor students. To improve academic achievement for students of color, it is important to challenge long-held assumptions about their abilities and the roles of the schools (Williams).

Along with being our largest and, on average, youngest group of minorities, Latinos are less likely than any other group of students to receive early childhood education, including preschool or Head Start. They are more likely to be enrolled below grade level and in remedial classes and have been retained one or more times. They have the highest dropout rate and are more likely to take courses that do not prepare them for college. Latino and African-American students are more likely to be categorized as low SES and to attend schools with a low Cumulative Promotion Index or Promoting Power Index.

Even when African-American students enter school with skills and knowledge equal to their Caucasian peers, they often finish elementary school with lower reading and vocabulary skills. Likewise, African-American students who enter high school with the same math, reading, science, and history scores as their Caucasian peers finish with lowered reading scores, and the gap increases by the end of high school for those who fell behind in elementary school (Phillips et al.).

Can Do. . .

How are vocabulary words displayed around the school library? Take a walk around the school. Is there an emphasis on building vocabulary in the hall displays? The lunchroom? Other common areas outside the classrooms? Visit <esl.about.com/library/ vocabulary/ blwordgroups_celebrations_other_e.htm> for great ideas on vocabulary activities for students who are learning English.

Students benefit academically when educators build on students' strengths and cultural capital (Thompson). A. Wade Boykin, a researcher at Howard University in Washington, D.C., has developed a model for improving the academic achievement of African-American students (and it is common sense that all students, regardless of their ethnicity or class, would benefit as well). His "additive pedagogy" model is unlike the traditional, middle-class model of schooling which uses a "talent-sorting, weeding-out approach." Boykin's model for improving academic achievement consists of the following eight components:

1. High standards for all students
2. Multiple ways to determine students' success
3. Approaches that build on students' assets
4. A developmentally appropriate education
5. An active, constructivist approach to learning
6. A thematic and interdisciplinary curriculum
7. Preparation for the demands of the twenty-first century
8. A caring school community focused on students' academic and personal well-being (Boykin 87)

Being in the minority at school challenges students' sense of belonging unless their ethnic identity is well developed and they see the majority culture in a positive light (Velasquez). According to Payne, schools are organized around middle class values. If the student experiences tension between their family's values or goals and the school's educational goals, then their sense of belonging is further challenged which may cause them to disconnect. When a student does not understand these middle class rules he may have a difficult time getting along at school or in the classroom (Payne).

Any discussion, however brief, about racially and ethnically diverse students must include individuals who are native to the United States—Indians, Eskimos, Aleutian Islanders, and Hawaiians. Over half of the Native-American population lives in five states: Alaska, Arizona, California, New Mexico, and Oklahoma. The majority of these students attend public schools where the enrollment of Native-American students is low. They are "caught between two cultures" (Smith 73). Smith points out that these students communicate differently at home than at school. At home, communication tends to be symbolic, unlike the verbal and direct style employed at school. For American Indian children, mainstream communication may be too aggressive, questioning too intrusive, and eye contact too direct. These students are among those who have the lowest SES, and have a dropout rate that is 25 percent higher than the national average.

Immigration

One of the greatest challenges facing educators today is the increase in immigrant students. Over the past 20 years, immigration has contributed to the dramatic increase in student diversity (Taylor and Whittaker). If current trends continue, by the year 2050 members of minority groups will make up approximately 40 percent of the population. According to research into effective schools and school reform, "a change in community demographics . . . requires modifications in the policies and practices for including families in the school community. What worked before becomes obsolete" (Zambone et al. 12). Schools are being challenged to change.

According to the United Nations, economic promise draws most families to the United States from some of the poorest countries in the world (Capps et. al.). Consequently, the increasing number of immigrant children is challenging schools and putting these students at risk for low achievement because they are poor and do not speak English—and because schools do not know how to serve them.

Sometimes immigrants stay in the place they first arrived, surrounded by friends and relatives who speak their language and understand their culture, but more and more frequently they are moving to other areas, as are U.S. citizens of color (Frey and DeVol). The states that currently have the fastest growing school-age immigrant population are located in the southeast, midwest, and interior west, with Nevada, North Carolina, Georgia, and Nebraska heading the list (Capps, et. al.). However, schools all over the United States are facing changing demographics as a result of immigration.

In 2000, 20 percent of children under the age of 18 were children of immigrants, although the majority of children whose parents were immigrants were born here in the U.S. (Gould and Findlay). Children of immigrants make up 25 percent of the students who have low socioeconomic status, as defined by the National School Lunch Program. The influx of immigrant children into the U.S. public school system has generated a great deal of concern about their school success and adaptation (Pong). Often, immigrant children are at a great disadvantage compared to Caucasian children because they are poorer, their parents have less education, there are deficiencies in English, and there is stress due to lack of jobs and health care.

To understand the educational success of immigrant children, Suet-ling Pong of the Population Research Institute of The Pennsylvania State University, examined the interrelationship between generations (first, second, and third) and race and ethnicity (Asian and Hispanic). His research indicates that Hispanics are the most disadvantaged in terms of socioeconomic status and attend schools with lower quality than those attended by Asians or Caucasians. Hispanics are more likely to attend highly urbanized schools with large dropout rates. Of Hispanics, Cuban students attend the most urbanized schools and have the highest dropout rates. With the exception of Vietnamese students, Asian minorities are over-represented in suburban and private schools. The Vietnamese were the only Asian group that had SES characteristics similar to Hispanic groups (Pong).

A second part of his research focused on the psychological measures of optimism in immigrant children. He found that Vietnamese and Central and South American students are less likely to believe they will live until 35 years of age. In general, African/Caribbean Americans and Hispanics are less optimistic about their longevity and earning a middle-class income by age 30. However, African/Caribbean American adolescents are more optimistic than European whites regarding graduating from college. Mexican students are least likely to believe they can graduate from college. By contrast, Asian students have the highest educational expectation of all racial/ethnic groups (Pong).

Think About. . .

Review your school library's holdings. How many books have themes about immigrant experiences? What other resources related to immigration are in the collection?

Limited English Proficiency (LEP)

Within the next five years, over 30 percent of students will come from homes where English is not the primary language. New York City's students and their families speak over two hundred languages; in Rochester, Minnesota over 60 languages are spoken in the schools. Even though many of these students are bilingual, proficient in English as well as the language of their home, they represent different stages of English language development. Deborah Short and Jane Echevarria note several factors that influence a student's proficiency in English and the ease with which they can learn it:

- Similarity of the native language to English; for instance, Spanish is more similar to English than is Arabic or Chinese
- Background knowledge and how it relates to what is being taught in school influences a student's ability to move from social English to academic English, or from the playground to the classroom
- Literacy and education levels of the family in their native language
- Previous education history and experience in their native country
- *Quality of the instruction received in their U.S. schools* (the most important factor according to the research)

This is such a diverse group in terms of their language abilities that it is wrong to assume they are fluent enough to learn curriculum content and build relationships in English based on their use of the language or the amount of time they have been in U.S. schools. Some students can clearly pronounce words that they do not understand, while others are able to communicate in English with peers but not with adults. Because students must learn the basic grammatical rules of a language before they learn to read and write it, many children may speak some English but are not literate. Each child, including those from the same family, comes to school with different language abilities and progresses at different rates.

Students learning to speak English often understand more than they can express. This leads adults to think that a student either has a better or worse grasp of the language than in fact he or she does. Additionally, their emotional state will affect students' ease with language—for example we all have trouble *using our words* when angry or deeply upset. Limited English proficient students are particularly vulnerable for low achievement because, in many schools, there are few accommodations in instruction or materials for a student's level of language development.

There are several approaches to teaching English. English as a Second Language (ESL) emphasizes learning and using English in the classroom and on preparing English Language Learners (ELL) to function in mainstream English-language classrooms. English Language Learners may be placed in an ESL class, sheltered English classes, or they may participate in a pullout ESL class.

The second approach is Traditional Bilingual Education (also sometimes referred to as early exit bilingual education). In this type of program, students' native language is used in classrooms to help students learn academic content while they are learning English. As soon as possible (usually within two or three years), students are moved into instruction in English only. The goal is proficiency in English, not continuing to develop the student's native language skills.

The third approach is Developmental Bilingual Education (also referred to as maintenance bilingual education or late exit bilingual education) which emphasizes developing and maintaining proficiency in students' native language as well as English. Students entering developmental bilingual programs as kindergartners are typically taught to read and write in their native language first, and then literacy skills are transferred to English. Once students function in both languages, they continue to learn language and content in both languages.

The fourth approach is Dual Language Education (also referred to as two-way bilingual or two-way immersion). These programs serve a mix of English Language Learners and native English-speaking students. They teach language and content in both English and in a target language (for example, Spanish, Japanese, and so on.). The goal is for all students to become literate in both English and the target language, and to develop and maintain both languages.

English language learners (also referred to as LEP or limited English proficiency) often face discrimination, failure, and isolation; their intellectual and social abilities are underestimated. Information—both academic and social—may be a problem when LEP students do not understand the language of instruction and cannot read social cues about expected behaviors. Older students are often shy, frustrated, and confused, which can make them appear troubled or withdrawn. Expectations and opportunities for LEP students are usually limited, unless they can shine in non-language based activities—and not many of these activities are valued in schools. The media center may be the one place, outside of an LEP classroom or resource room, where LEP students can read materials that interest them at their own pace or otherwise use their native language. These students are vulnerable for low achievement because, in many schools, there is little individual accommodation in instruction or materials for a student's level of language development.

We often mistakenly assume that students who are not fluent in English have a disability, while we miss others who are disabled. Test results can grossly under-represent their abilities and achievement. Students who are not Caucasian, particularly those who are LEP, are under-represented in programs for gifted and talented learners, and over-represented in special education.

Special Education

Students receiving special education services have lower graduation rates than any other population. For example, according to the 2000 Annual Report to Congress on Implementation of IDEA, the high school graduation rate for typical students was 50.2 percent for African Americans, 53.2 percent for Latinos, and 51.1 percent for American Indian/Alaskan Native students, while only 43% of special education students graduated in the same year (Orfield, et al.).

The percentage of students in gifted or special education should reflect their presence in the larger population. However, this is not happening. When we compare the percentage of children in these programs to demographic counts, all groups except for Caucasian and Asian students either are under- or over-represented (Orfield, et. al.).

This problem of under- or over-representation has two aspects. First, schools do not correctly identify the disabilities of some students at risk for low achievement or failure. Other at-risk students are not disabled but end up in special education solely based on low achievement. Over-representation of students of color in special education, particularly African-American students in the categories of mild mental retardation (MMR) and behavior/emotional disorders (BED) has been a concern for many years. Figure 2.1 shows the percentage of each population (POP) according to the 2000 U.S. Census, and the percentage in Special Education (SE) according to the 2000 Annual Report to Congress on the Implementation of the Individuals with Disabilities Act (IDEA). To learn more about over-representation and other issues of equity in education go to <www.civilrightsproject.harvard.edu>.

Figure 2.1: Ethnicity in the General School Population in Special Education

ETHNICITY IN THE GENERAL SCHOOL POPULATION AND SPECIAL EDUCATION									
American Indian/ Alaska Native		Asian/Pacific Islander		African American		Latino/ Hispanic		Caucasian	
POP	SE	POP	SE	POP	SE	POP	SE	POP	SE
.07	1.3	3.7	1.8	12.1	20.3	12.5	13.7	69.5	62.9

Source: Twenty-Fifth Annual Report to Congress on the Implementation of the Individuals with Disabilities Education Act (2003). For the complete report, go to <www.ed.gov/about/reports/annual/osep/2003>.

The disability categories and labels of MMR and BED are often described as "socially constructed," which means that students are labeled disabled in one setting such as school, but not in another. Low-SES students who are racially, ethnically, and linguistically diverse are often labeled disabled because their ways of interacting with teachers and schools are different (Cummins).

Lloyd Dunn first coined the term "six-hour retarded child" in the 1960s. He described those students, predominantly African American, who were considered mentally retarded by the school, but went home to be successful in after-school jobs, with friendships in their neighborhoods, and in their chores at home.

Another group of students misplaced in special education are those with Attention Deficit Disorder (ADD) or Attention Deficit Hyperactivity Disorder (ADHD). These students may act impulsively. Sometimes they find their surroundings distracting. At other times they focus so intently on something that captures their attention that they have trouble moving on to other tasks. Because their ways of learning and focusing their attention do not match the instructional style of the majority, these students often end up misplaced in special education programs for children labeled behavior/emotionally disordered.

Even when students are eligible for special education services there are several reasons why this designation is disadvantageous. The first is the stigma associated with the labels. Second, students identified as disabled are victims of lower expectations and provided fewer opportunities for success. Third, despite legislation and other efforts to promote inclusion, they often do not participate in the general education classroom. The result is that students have fewer opportunities to interact with their peers as equals and to learn the standard curriculum, which intensifies the stigma and low expectations associated with disability.

In other cases being identified as special education benefits students who otherwise would not receive the supports, accommodations, and specialized instruction that they need. Many students with disabilities are reluctant to take risks and give up trying to learn despite their potential, so providing motivation and building self-esteem are as important as academic content and skills. To learn more about different disabilities visit the web site for the Council for Exceptional Children at <www.cec.sped.org>.

Think About. . .

Why do you think that the school library is often the place where students who struggle with behavior or learning in the classroom are successful? Ask this question of teachers who bring their class to the library or send troublesome children to work in there.

Another growing group of vulnerable students who may, or may not, be served by special education are students who experience trauma. In the U.S. each year as many as five million students experience an extreme trauma (Perry). Trauma includes witnessing a violent event or an accident, severe illness and painful medical treatments, experiencing a natural or man-made disaster, or abuse. According to Perry, nearly 40% of this group will develop long-term neuropsychological disorders that can impair their academic, social, and emotional functioning. In some cases, school personnel may know that the child is traumatized, in others they may not. Students who are low SES, those with disabilities, immigrants, LEP, and students of color are particularly vulnerable to trauma.

Children respond differently to trauma depending on the severity, duration, and pattern of the event; their resiliency; the support offered following the experience; age; stage of development; and previous experience with trauma. Trauma alters a child's emotional and cognitive response to the world. If trauma occurs at a young age, particularly if it is both extreme and ongoing, it can alter brain development. Children who have experienced trauma may appear to have learning disabilities or ADD/ADHD. They may be depressed, which often manifests as anger and aggression. Often they will do anything in their power to keep themselves safe. Children's intense feelings of trauma may be reactivated from time to time if something happens to remind them of the event. For instance, if the trauma occurred when it was raining, then the child might experience the same feelings of trauma every time it rains.

Children's efforts to keep themselves safe and maintain an emotional and physical balance are often hard to understand or tolerate in school. They may become angry, withdrawn, or have ADD/ADHD symptoms. These children may have no problem behaviors until something triggers the feeling and memory associated with the trauma. It is only when school personnel and families look back that they realize that outbursts occurred, for instance, on a rainy day, or when there was a fire drill.

Children who experience trauma primarily need a sense of safety and control over their world. It takes time to manage feelings and make sense of the event. This is particularly true if a family member or other trusted adult perpetrated the trauma. They may require short- or long-term therapy. Media specialists can create a safe haven for these students, regain their trust, help them put their experience in perspective, and play a role in restoring resiliency and reversing their trajectory toward failure.

Think About. . .

Children feel safe when they know what to expect, that rules will be in place and enforced consistently, and that they and other students will receive the attention and help they need to be successful. Review the rules and procedures in the school library to see how it can be a place where students feel safe.

Often the media center is the one place where special education students participate in the life of their school. The resources, environment, and support offered there can provide a context for these students to be successful. In later chapters we will provide suggestions and strategies for engaging students with disabilities, particularly those students whose disabilities may only be evident in the classroom and those students with conditions like ADD/ADHD.

Resources to Learn More about This Topic

"A Culturally Relevant Lesson for African American Students," by Mary Stone Hanley at <www.newhorizons.org/strategies/multicultural/hanley2.htm> identifies strategies that engage students in learning.

The Multicultural Education Web site at <www.newhorizons.org/strategies/multicultural/ front_multicultural.htm> provides background information and strategies to use with a diverse student body. From this site there is a link to information about special needs children at <www.newhorizons.org/strategies/multicultural/front_multicultural.htm>.

For more information on traumatized students, <www.childtrauma.com> provides information and resources for those who work with trauma-exposed children, adolescents, and adults.

The Web site <www.psy.pdx.edu/PsiCafe/KeyTheorists/EcoApp.htm> provides information about the ecological perspective and its application to education.

For more information on at-risk students and how schools are responding to this population, go to <www.ed.gov/nclb/overview/welcome/closing/index.html> and <www.civilrightsproject.harvard.edu>.

For access to the work of the regional education laboratories, a network of regional groups producing ideas, discussions of issues, and other resources for families, school personnel, and others on supporting diverse and at-risk students, including model programs and effective strategies, go to <www.relnetwork.org/>. You can link to each region's group from there.

For information and ideas for working with limited English proficient students, go to <www.bankstreet.edu/literacyguide/ell.html>.

For a copy of the Short and Echevarria article and more ideas on how to help LEP students, visit <www.barrow.k12.ga.us/esol/Teacher_Skills_to_Support_English_Language _Learners.pdf>.

CHAPTER THREE

Legislation and Effective Schools

Despite over 40 years of legislative efforts to resolve the conditions that place students at risk for low achievement and school failure, America is facing a crisis in education. Often, we blame *No Child Left Behind* (NCLB) and other legislation, such as *Individuals with Disabilities Education Act* (IDEA) for the increasing decline of education for at-risk students; however, these laws are not the problem, although regulations and procedures for implementing them may obscure their intent that children receive a high quality, appropriate education. Although some regulations pose financial and logistical challenges, these laws can empower families and communities, requiring schools to engage them in the issues that are continuing the cycle of failure for many students. The laws also can provide a framework for quality educational services for all students—standards, supports, individualized education, research-based practice, and meaningful assessment (Duttweiler).

It is more appropriate to address resistance to change, rather than complain about standards. While "powerful systemic forces and resistance to change can maintain the status quo . . . powerful forces can also be mustered to support comprehensive school reform" (Duttweiler 62). Examples of school reform abound. One example is that the NCLB legislation extends to families the right to move their child to successful schools. A second example is that IDEA requires parents to participate on the team that plans their child's education and services, and grants them due process if opportunities to do so are not forthcoming. In this way, these laws provide the impetus to overcome "powerful systemic forces" and make the changes necessary to both set high standards and implement education programs that will make it possible for students to meet them (Drew 68).

All school personnel have the responsibility to meet the intent and the letter of the laws that govern education. The intent of these laws, despite how it feels some days, is not to make things more difficult. Rather, they represent an ongoing effort to reverse the failure of at-risk students. Because media specialists are often in a position to form relationships with students and support their learning in creative and motivating ways, laws can help supply the impetus to advocate for low-achieving students and provide the rationale for doing things in new or different ways to help students who otherwise might not succeed.

Education Laws and At-Risk Students

The Tenth Amendment cites the responsibility of each state to provide the services and supports not specifically provided for in the federal law (Yell and Draskow). Historically, education was the responsibility of each state and they set their own standards and designed their own education systems. The federal government has increased its role in response to changes in student populations and growing numbers of at-risk students and has attempted to reform education through legislation to more effectively meet the needs of at-risk students. Two major efforts which began decades ago that affect schools today are the *Elementary and Secondary Education Act* of 1965 (ESEA) now called *No Child Left Behind Act* (NCLB); and the *Education of the Handicapped Act* of 1975, currently called the *Individuals with Disabilities Education Act* (IDEA).

Elementary and Secondary Education Act/No Child Left Behind

In 1965, the federal government passed ESEA to address problems of growing enrollment, increasing poverty and cultural diversity, segregation, and fragmented school systems. ESEA was the first major education law that increased the federal government's role by providing large amounts of funding and legislating standards for quality schools. Figure 3.1 shows the major provision of ESEA and the ways it attempted to address social problems.

Figure 3.1: Major Provisions of the *Elementary and Secondary Education Act*

MAJOR PROVISION OF THE ELEMENTARY AND SECONDARY EDUCATION ACT	
Title I	Upgrade the quality of education for poor and culturally diverse children
Title II	Provided for school libraries, textbooks and materials
Title III	Development of innovative or supplementary resource centers for schools
Title IV	Grants for research and development
Title V	Strengthen state education agencies

Source: U.S. Department of Education. For the complete legislation, go to <www.ed.gov/policy/elsec/leg/esea02/beginning>.

As students continue to fail, legislative efforts at school reform persist. In 1983, the federal Commission on Excellence in Education, in its report *A Nation At Risk,* recommended higher standards because American students were falling increasingly further behind students in other countries. States worked diligently to meet the report's recommendations. By 1990 the National Center for Education

Statistics (NCES) reported that nearly 40 percent of high school students met the tougher standards set by *A Nation At Risk* (Yell and Drasgow).

In 1989, at the first Governor's Education Summit, the 50 governors identified six educational goals that became part of the *America 2000* education legislation and the centerpiece for *Goals 2000: Educate America Act*. This act created the Education Standards and Improvement Council, which had the authority to review and accept or reject the academic standards set by each state. Although Congress disbanded the Council, the 1994 reauthorization of ESEA, *Improving America's Schools Act*, required standards-based education in all schools.

No Child Left Behind (NCLB), the 2001 reauthorization of ESEA, went further than the original ESEA legislation, or any other education law since, in expanding the role of the federal government and increasing government funding. It is a massive and complex piece of legislation consisting of ten titles or sections, in contrast to only five that made up the original version of ESEA. *No Child Left Behind* statutes and a PDF version of the law are available at <www.ed.gov/policy/elsec/leg/esea02/ index.html>.

The primary purpose of NCLB "is to ensure that all children have a fair, equal, and significant opportunity to obtain a high-quality education, and reach, at a minimum, proficiency on challenging state academic achievement standards and state academic assessments." Specifically, NCLB requires states to:

- Ensure that highly qualified teachers are in every classroom
- Use research-based practices as the foundation of instruction
- Develop tests to assess students so that data-driven decisions become an integral part of the educational system
- Hold schools accountable for performance of all students (Yell and Drasgow 2-3)

Accountability is the central theme of NCLB. This includes identifying standards of learning and assessing students' progress in meeting them. NCLB requires use of research-based teaching practices and curricula. All school personnel, not just teachers, must attain high qualifications for their role. Out-of-field teaching or otherwise not being adequately prepared for a role is strictly limited. Figure 3.2 provides an overview NCLB provisions.

Figure 3.2: Major Provisions of the *No Child Left Behind Act*

MAJOR PROVISIONS OF THE NO CHILD LEFT BEHIND ACT	
Title I	Improving academic achievement of the disadvantaged
Title II	Preparing, training, and recruiting high quality teachers
Title III	Language instruction for limited English proficient and immigrant students
Title IV	21st Century Schools – Safe, drug-free, and tobacco free with 21st Century Learning Centers
Title V	Promoting informed parental choice and innovative programs
Title VI	Flexibility and accountability
Title VII	Indian, native Hawaiian, and Alaskan native education
Title VIII	Impact aid program
Title IX	General provisions (e.g. flexible use of funds, definitions, waivers)
Title X	Repeals, redesignations, and amendments to other statutes

(Adapted from Yell and Drasgow 11-12)

Source: U.S. Department of Education. For the complete legislation, go to <www.ed.gov/about/offices/list/oese/legislation.html>.

Media specialists are one important key to schools meeting the spirit and the letter of NCLB. Like classroom teachers, they should be qualified for their role and engage in ongoing professional development, provide high quality materials and resources through the school library, collaborate with teachers, identify and implement effective research-based practices, and help students develop the research skills and concepts needed to meet high educational standards.

Can Do. . .

Visit the What Works Clearing House at <www.whatworks.ed.gov> to explore the different strategies and approaches that are proving to be effective, such as the *Talent Search* that helps middle and high school students complete school. Find one idea you can implement in the school library—for example, *Talent Search* helps middle school students learn about and connect with colleges. Think about creating a college exploration game where students look up different universities and post interesting facts and pictures.

Education of the Handicapped Act/ Individuals with Disabilities Education Act

The *Education of the Handicapped Act* (EHA) of 1976 confirmed the right of children with disabilities to a free, appropriate, public education. EHA, as a civil rights act, has its roots in Section 504 of the *Vocational Rehabilitation Act* of 1973, which prohibited discrimination against people with disabilities in any program or activity that received federal funding. EHA resulted from the advocacy of families and others whose children were excluded from school because of their disabilities.

Over the years, EHA has evolved to address problems in special education, including a change to people-first language in its name—*Individuals with Disabilities Education Act* (IDEA). Along with a free, appropriate public education and federal funding to help states provide special education services (often referred to as FAPE), IDEA clearly identifies procedures for placing students outside of the general education classroom; streamlines procedures for deciding who is eligible for special education and for discipline; sets standards for access to technology for these students; and clarifies the meaning and criteria for identifying students as disabled in each category (e.g. Mental Retardation, Learning Disabled, and Emotional Disorders).

IDEA requires the following:

- Rights of Due Process: Parents are informed and must participate in development of their child's programs according to a prescribed timeline and set of procedures. Parents have the right to a hearing in the event there is disagreement.
- Individualized Education Plans: Individualized education and services for all children with disabilities.
- Related Services: Services deemed necessary to enable the child to participate in and benefit from their education, such as speech and language therapy and physical therapy.
- Non-Discriminatory Assessment: Assessment in the student's primary language, using instruments whose norms are based on individuals of the same racial, ethnic, socioeconomic, and regional group as the child being tested.
- Least Restrictive Environment: Education provided to the fullest extent possible in general education, unless schools can demonstrate that another setting is the least restrictive environment. This is often referred to as LRE.
- Comprehensive System of Personnel Development: Each state must submit a plan for providing professional development and training to all school personnel (including media specialists) to meet the needs of students with disabilities.
- Interdisciplinary Team: A team that includes the parent and the general educator must conduct assessment and educational planning.

A major change to the 2004 reauthorization of IDEA is the role of general education. Now students' goals and benchmarks must relate to the general education standards. It is mandatory for general education teachers to participate in every facet of determining whether a student is eligible for special education services. IDEA also requires a pre-referral process. Before testing a student to determine if he or she has a disability that is interfering with their success, the general educator must consult with families, specialists, and colleagues to attempt to resolve the behavioral or learning challenges by making changes in the classroom environment and instruction. Media specialists can play an important role in this process because of their knowledge of resources and technology. The school library is often a place where students who are not successful in the classroom feel welcome and can find materials that are meaningful and useful to them. If the student continues to need extra help after those changes have been made, then the school develops the Individualized Education Plan (IEP).

The IEP is the contract the school makes with the student and family describing the services, accommodations, and supports the student will receive. The IEP also describes the goals and benchmarks that the student will achieve during the year because of these services. For example, if a student is very severely visually impaired, the IEP may require access to reading devices, computer software, and Braille materials in the media center. If the student has a behavioral or emotional disability, the IEP may specify that he can work in the media center when the classroom is too stressful.

Media specialists are responsible for providing the supports, adaptations, and modifications mandated in a student's IEP as they relate to their use of the media center. They may consult on a pre-referral team that is supporting the general education teacher, provide some of the services that help a child achieve a goal, and offer input into the assessment process based on their knowledge of the student and how he functions in the center. For example, if a student has a vocational goal, he or she may work in the media center shelving books or performing other services. The special education teacher, together with the media specialist, is responsible for supporting the student's achievement of that goal.

An additional requirement in the IDEA revisions addresses dropout prevention. In 2002, the most recent year that data is available, only 51% of students with disabilities completed school with a standard diploma. IDEA requires states to collect data on dropout and graduation rates as a first step toward developing effective dropout prevention programs that include students with disabilities. Many of the special education students who are capable of attaining a high school diploma but do not complete school are those at risk for misidentification as special needs (discussed in Chapter Two) because of race or poverty. Any efforts to increase the resiliency of students needs to include students receiving special education services.

Section 504 of the Vocational and Rehabilitation Act *and the* Americans with Disabilities Act

There are laws that address specific aspects of education. For example, the *Reading Excellence Act* of 1999 provides incentives for state and local school districts to improve their literacy programs. Other laws, while not focused on schools, have direct implications for them. Two examples are Section 504 of the *Vocational Rehabilitation Act*, and the *Americans with Disabilities Act* (ADA), which is an outgrowth of Section 504. These laws address the civil rights of individuals with disabilities regarding access and freedom from discrimination. Because not all students with disabilities require special education services and because the disability criteria in these two laws are broader than IDEA, students who might not be served by special education but require accommodations such as wheelchair ramps, special devices, or untimed testing may have a 504 plan.

Knowing which students have 504 plans and the kinds of accommodations they require are important for media specialists if they are to ensure that all students can benefit from the services they provide. One student may require books on tape, while another requires a special joystick or keyboard on the computer. An important aspect of these two laws, as well as IDEA, is the accessibility of physical facilities. Students with physical and sensory disabilities must have equal access, which includes ensuring that they can enter and use the resources of the school library as independently as students without disabilities. This includes features such as automatic doors, Braille labels wherever print labels are provided, ramps, accessible storage of materials, and available technology to enlarge print, read print, and record information.

Think About...

Ask to see several IEPs and 504 plans and have the process explained to you. As you review these educational plans, consider where you could fit in. For instance, if a student is having specific reading difficulties, how could you and the school library program's resources and services support this student's academic achievement?

Resources to Learn More about This Topic

American Library Association. *Your School Library Media Program and No Child Left Behind.* 2004. Chicago, IL. 26 Jan. 2007 <www.ala.org/ala/aaslbucket/ AASLNCLBBrochureweb.pdf>.

"Close Up: NCLB—Improving Literacy through School Libraries." NCLB: The Achiever 15 Sep. 2004 <www.ed.gov/news/newsletters/ achiever/2004/091504.html>.

NCLB is highly controversial. Visit <www.civilrightsproject.harvard.edu> to read several research studies and policy analyses outlining strengths and concerns about the law. Education of students with disabilities is one of the controversies surrounding NCLB.

To view your state's NCLB Accountability Plan view "approved state's accountability plans" at <www.ed.gov/admins/lead/account/stateplans>.

To view IDEA and resources related to IDEA, visit <www.ed.gov/offices/ OSERS/ IDEA>.

The federal government's role in education is described at <www.ed.gov/ about/overview/fed/role.html>.

A Nation At Risk archived report can be found at www.ed.gov/pubs/ NatAtRisk/risk.html>.

To learn more about how to support students with special needs visit <www. ideapractices.org>.

To learn more about the accessibility requirements for school libraries and other facilities visit <www.access-board.gov/ada-aba>.

SECTION TWO

What Is Effective?

Introduction

Research described in this next section makes it clear that school libraries improve student achievement, effective schools and teachers make a difference, specific instructional practices lead to success, and connecting with students is important. The purpose of this section is to present research-based findings that bring life to the media specialist's vision of a school library program which is integral to building an effective school. Figure 4.1 illustrates the impact of effective schools.

Figure 4.1: Effective Versus Ineffective Schools, Assuming 20 Percent of Variance

EFFECTIVE VERSUS INEFFECTIVE SCHOOLS, ASSUMING 20 PERCENT VARIANCE		
Group	Outcome	
	Percentage of Students Who Pass the Test	Percentage of Students Who Fail the Test
Effective Schools	72.4%	27.6%
Ineffective Schools	27.6%	72.4%

Source: Marzano, Robert. J. (2003). *What Works in School: Translating Research into Action*. Alexandria, VA: Association for Supervision and Curriculum Development. Reprinted by Permission. The Association for Supervision and Curriculum Development is a worldwide community of educators advocating sound policies and sharing best practices to achieve the success of each learner. To learn more, visit ASCD at <www.ascd.org>.

Research shows there are a core number of instructional and behavioral practices and strategies that lead to student success. In this section media specialists will recognize how this research is interrelated and the ways in which it is applicable to everyone in the school community, regardless of their role or profession. For instance, resiliency research conducted by Emmy E. Werner and Ruth Smith provides evidence that mentoring is a powerful strategy to help troubled youth develop feelings of worth and set goals that lead to a brighter future. In their research, teachers were often described as mentors who listened and provided guidance. However, mentoring is also a strategy for increasing students' background knowledge—which increases vocabulary, the building block for reading.

In Chapter Four, the impact study research conducted by Lance, Welborn, Hamilton-Pennell, Rodney, and others will be briefly reviewed. This chapter provides a general overview of findings rather than a detailed review of the results of each study because this information is readily available in articles, books, and on Web sites. In Chapter Five, specific research-based strategies will be presented.

CHAPTER FOUR

The Impact Study Research: School Library Characteristics That Raise Academic Achievement

In the past 60 years or so, approximately 75 studies have concluded that school library programs lead to increased student academic achievement (Lonsdale 11). Although these studies reflect diverse research focuses, employ various methodologies, and investigate a range of grade levels in the United States as well as abroad, their findings consistently show that school libraries with a media specialist at the helm result in improved learning and cognition.

Think About...

Visit the Impact Studies page of the Library Research Service Web site at <www.lrs.org/impact.asp> and read the reports and presentations. Conduct an informal assessment of your school library program to determine how it matches up with the impact study findings. In what areas is the school library program strong? In what areas is the school library program lacking? The next step is to develop a plan to strengthen the areas that are lacking.

Although early studies provided evidence that a school's library program benefits students' academic achievement, it is the body of research known as impact studies conducted by Lance and his colleagues that decisively prove the connection between the two. Michele Lonsdale writes in a review of impact study research for the Australian Council for Educational Research that the "most influential body of research into the impact of school libraries on student achievement is that of Keith Curry Lance and his colleagues" (12).

The first impact study conducted by Lance and his colleagues, *Impact of School Library Media Centers on Academic Achievement: 1993 Colorado Study*, "identified the importance of the library media specialist playing an instructional role in the school, but it did not define what that meant and what it involved doing"

(Lance, *Impact* 30). Although the findings of this study also implied the value of principal and teacher support, it did not address these issues directly. Furthermore, this study did not demonstrate the important relationship of information technology to the library media program. This study has come to be known as the first Colorado study because it was followed up by a second state study in 2000 which did establish these important connections.

However, what the first Colorado study did find was that the size of a school library's staff and collection is the best school predictor of academic achievement on standardized tests. According to the study, students who score higher on norm-referenced tests tend to come from schools with larger media staff, more books, more periodicals, and more videos (Lance et al.). The media specialist contributes to student achievement by shaping the school library collection, collaborating with classroom teachers, and providing leadership.

The methodology of the first Colorado study has been revised and repeated by Lance and his colleagues in Alaska, Pennsylvania, Colorado, and Oregon to determine if "the claimed relationships between library media programs and student performance exist when a state's standardized tests are substituted for norm-referenced tests" such as the Iowa Test of Basic Skills (Lance, *Impact* 30). This methodology fostered studies in other states beyond those identified above, including Florida, Massachusetts, and North Carolina, to determine the connection between academic achievement and the school library. Figure 4.2 graphically displays the specific characteristics of effective school libraries.

Figure 4.2 How School Librarians Help Kids Achieve Standards: The Second Colorado Study

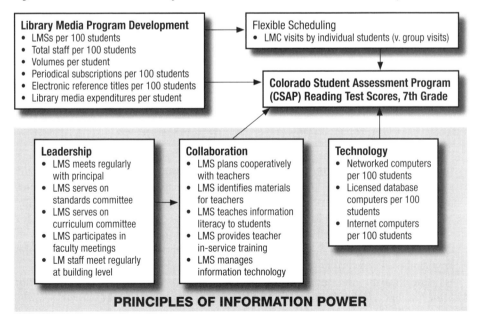

Source: Lance, Keith Curry, Marcia J. Rodney, and Christine Hamilton-Pennell, *How School Librarians Help Kids Achieve Standards: The Second Colorado Study,* Salt Lake City: Hi Willow Research. Reprinted by Permission.

A distinguishing feature of the Lance methodology is that it controls for social and community variables whereas earlier studies did not. Studies without sufficient controls resulted in uncertainty about the role of the library program in raising student achievement. Lance acknowledges this limitation and writes: "For instance, when it was found that higher library media expenditures correlated with higher test scores, it was easy to explain away this relationship by attributing the test scores to higher school expenditures generally" (*Impact* 33).

As shown in Chapter Two of this book, socioeconomic status (SES) is the most significant predictor for high school dropout and low student achievement. Lance and his colleagues found that after accounting for socioeconomic status, "library media predictors almost always outperformed other school characteristics, such as teacher-pupil ratio and per pupil expenditures" in improving student achievement (*Impact* 34). The message for media specialists is that an effective school library benefits students and this finding needs to be presented to school district administrators, principals, and teachers.

Can Do...

Present the discussed impact evidence to the teachers and principal at your school. You can use the U.S. Department of Education's report *School Library Media Center: Selected Results from the Educational Longitudinal Study of 2002* at <nces.ed.gov/pubsearch/pubsinfo.asp?pubid=2005302> as a source of information for your presentation.

Lance identifies the following trends from impact study research conducted in Alaska, Pennsylvania, Colorado, Oregon, Iowa, and New Mexico indicating that students' academic performance improves when the following occurs:

- The media specialist plans and collaborates with classroom teachers to deliver instruction, teaches information literacy, and works one-on-one tutoring students in a flexible environment
- The media specialist develops and manages quality collections to support the curriculum
- State-of-the-art technology is integrated into the learning and teaching processes
- The media specialist cooperates between school and other types of libraries, especially public libraries
- The school library is staffed by a professional media specialist and assisted by support personnel
- The principal supports the school library program
- Collaboration occurs between the media specialist and teachers

- Information technology extends the reach of the school library program into classrooms and labs
- A well-organized and formally requested budget is allocated to support the above conditions (Hamilton-Pennell, et al.)

Other studies show that students benefit when school librarians teach information literacy skills to students, collaborate with teachers, implement flexible scheduling, and utilize technology. A study conducted by Topsy N. Smalley, an instructional librarian at Cabrillo College in Aptos, California, found that "students whose high schools include librarians and library instruction programs bring more understanding about information research to their college experiences" (197).

A different approach to identify the impact of the school library on academic achievement was employed by Ross Todd and Carol Kuhlthau (Todd). Commonly referred to as the Ohio study, over 13,000 students in grades three through twelve were surveyed between October 2002 through December 2003 in order "to understand how school libraries specifically help young people with their learning" (Whelan 47). Todd and Kuhlthau's qualitative research differs from the quantitative methodology of Lance and his colleagues. Whereas the focus of the latter research was to identify the relationship between test scores and school library and school data, the Ohio study evaluated media centers based on how students responded to 48 statements. Schools that met certain criteria related to effective media centers—such as having a strong collection and a certified school librarian—were chosen to participate in a Web-based survey which resulted in 10,000 written responses about the helpfulness and usefulness of the media program. Students frequently wrote about the value of information literacy instruction and library-based classes that helped them to use and access information for research assignments. This study showed that school libraries are "actively engaged as learning instructional centers to develop intellectual scaffolds for students and to help them engage with information meaningfully to construct their own understanding of the topic they're studying" (Whelan 48).

Todd and Kuhlthau found that a proactive media specialist is imperative for a successful school library. However, there were other interesting findings. First, students rank general reading interests as sixth in order of importance and perceived computer technology to be a more important function of the school library. Second, girls consider school libraries as more helpful than do boys. Third, the school library has a greater impact on reading improvement for African-American students than for any other group (Whelan 48).

As previously stated, the intent of this chapter is not to review individual state findings but to present an overview of those factors that, in more than one state study, have been determined to increase student achievement. Although a researcher could argue that a finding in one state or school library does not automatically apply to another, there are commonalities that are too strong to overlook and should become part of the media specialist's plan to improve the school library program, thus increasing student achievement.

Learning and Teaching

The Information Power Vision Committee identified ten learning and teaching principles of school library media programs, which were approved by the American Association of School Librarians and the Association for Educational Communications and Technology. Figure 4.3 presents these principles.

Figure 4.3 Learning and Teaching Principles of School Library Media Programs

LEARNING AND TEACHING PRINCIPLES OF SCHOOL LIBRARY MEDIA PROGRAMS

Principle 1: The library media program is essential to learning and teaching and must be fully integrated into the curriculum to promote students' achievement of learning goals.

Principle 2: The information literacy standards for student learning are integral to the content and objectives of the school's curriculum.

Principle 3: The library media program models and promotes collaborative planning and curriculum development.

Principle 4: The library media program models and promotes creative, effective, and collaborative teaching.

Principle 5: Access to the full range of information resources and services through the library media program is fundamental to learning.

Principle 6: The library media program encourages and engages students in reading, viewing, and listening for understanding and enjoyment.

Principle 7: The library media program supports the learning of all students and other members of the learning community who have diverse learning abilities, styles, and needs.

Principle 8: The library media program fosters individual and collaborative inquiry.

Principle 9: The library media program integrates the uses of technology for learning and teaching.

Principle 10: The library media program is an essential link to the larger learning community.

These principles were identified and developed by the information Power Vision Committee, reviewed and commented upon by the profession, and approved by the AASL and AECT Boards as the cardinal premises on which learning and teaching within the effective school library media program is based.

Source. American Association of School Librarians and the Association for Educational Communications and Technology, *Information Power: Building Partnerships for Learning* p. 58, copyright 1998. Reprinted by Permission.

The impact study research identified two important qualities, or dispositions, of the media specialist that correlate with improved academic achievement. The first is leadership. The second is collaboration. According to Lance and David V. Loertscher, an indirect relationship exists between the two and "leadership translates to higher collaboration with teachers in creating quality learning experiences that in turn, have a direct impact on academic achievement" (48). A media specialist who recognizes the importance of leadership and collaboration, and how this translates into improved academic achievement, is more likely to focus on developing these two qualities.

Leadership The following five leadership qualities correlate with improved student achievement:

- Meets regularly with administrators
- Serves on standards committees
- Serves on curriculum committees
- Attends school staff meetings
- Holds library staff meetings (assuming more than a one-person staff) (Lance and Loertscher 48)

Collaboration Similar to leadership, collaboration leads to improved student achievement and is implemented in the following ways:

- Planning units together
- Identifying materials for teachers
- Teaching information literacy to learners
- Providing inservice training for teachers
- Providing motivational reading activities
- Pushing digital information beyond the LMC (Lance and Loertscher 29)

In addition, the two following factors have been shown to benefit student achievement:

- **Information Literacy** Teach information literacy skills that are integrated into curriculum and aligned with state curriculum standards, providing a "coherent instructional framework"
- **Inservice Training** Provide training that will help teachers understand and design lessons enriched with information literacy, technology, and information resources (Lance and Loertscher 95)

Information Access and Delivery

The Information Power Vision Committee identified seven information access and delivery principles of school library media programs, which were approved by the

American Association of School Librarians and the Association for Educational Communications and Technology. Figure 4.4 presents these principles.

Figure 4.4 Information Access and Delivery Principles of School Library Media Programs

INFORMATION ACCESS AND DELIVERY PRINCIPLES OF SCHOOL LIBRARY MEDIA PROGRAMS

Principle 1: The library media program provides intellectual access to information and ideas for learning.

Principle 2: The library media program provides physical access to information and resources for learning.

Principle 3: The library media program provides a climate that is conducive to learning.

Principle 4: The library media program requires flexible and equitable access to information, ideas, and resources for learning.

Principle 5: The collections of the library media program are developed and evaluated collaboratively to support the school's curriculum and to meet the diverse learning needs of students.

Principle 6: The library media program is founded on a commitment to the right of intellectual freedom.

Principle 7: The information policies, procedures, and practices of the library media program reflect legal guidelines and professional ethics.

These principles were identified and developed by the information Power Vision Committee, reviewed and commented upon by the profession, and approved by the AASL and AECT Boards as the cardinal premises on which learning and teaching within the effective school library media program is based.

Source: American Association of School Librarians and the Association for Educational Communications and Technology, *Information Power: Building Partnerships for Learning p. 83*, copyright 1998. Reprinted by Permission.

The findings of the impact study research clearly identified the importance of developing and maintaining a school library that provides students and educational stakeholders (teachers, staff, administrators, and perhaps parents) with full access to the resources of the school library program and beyond. According to these studies, the following information access and delivery factors were identified as leading to improved student achievement:

- Technology: Develop and support computer networks that provide access to information resources such as licensed databases and the Internet and can be utilized from classrooms and home
- Collection development: Current and larger collections of information resources such as books, periodicals, and databases; and policies that address the issues of reconsideration requests or challenges
- Increased access to school library: Open to students before and after school and during the day because of flexible scheduling
- Increased library services: Reference, interlibrary loan, reading guidance, and teaching information skills

Program Administration

The Information Power Vision Committee identified program administration principles of school library media programs, which were approved by the American Association of School Librarians and the Association for Educational Communications and Technology. Figure 4.5 presents these principles.

Figure 4.5 Program Administration Principles of School Library Media Programs

PROGRAM ADMINISTRATION PRINCIPLES OF SCHOOL LIBRARY MEDIA PROGRAMS

Principle 1: The library media program supports the mission, goals, objectives, and continuous improvement of the school.

Principle 2: In every school, a minimum of one full-time, certified/licensed library media specialist supported by qualified staff is fundamental to the implementation of an effective library media program at the building level.

Principle 3: An effective library media program requires a level of professional and support staffing that is based upon a school's instructional programs, services, facilities, size, and numbers of students and teachers.

Principle 4: An effective library media program requires ongoing administrative support.

Principle 5: Comprehensive and collaborative long-range, strategic planning is essential to the effectiveness of the library media program.

Principle 6: Ongoing assessment for improvement is essential to the vitality of an effective library media program.

Principle 7: Sufficient funding is fundamental to the success of the library media program.

Principle 8: Ongoing staff development—both to maintain professional knowledge and skills and to provide instruction in information literacy for teachers, administrators, and other members of the learning community—is an essential component of the library media program.

Principle 9: Clear communication of the mission, goals, functions and impact of the library media program is necessary to the effectiveness of the program.

Principle 10: Effective management of human, financial, and physical resources undergirds a strong library media program.

Source: American Association of School Librarians and the Association for Educational Communications and Technology, *Information Power: Building Partnerships for Learning* p. 100, copyright 1998. Reprinted by Permission.

The management, training, and advocacy functions of the media specialist are vital if the school library program is to have the human, financial, and physical resources needed to improve student achievement. According to the impact study research, this is accomplished in the following ways:

- Library staffing: A professionally trained and credentialed media specialist makes a difference, as does having support staff to free the media specialist to teach and collaborate with other educators

- Relationship with other libraries: A relationship—formal or informal—with the public library
- Budget: Formal and well-developed budget that is presented to the administrator; higher expenditures correlate with increased academic achievement
- Flexible access: Individual, not group, visits to the library are more likely to indicate that students are pursuing self-directed learning in which they are exercising information literacy skills
- Exercise of leadership: For example, meeting with the principal; participating in faculty and curriculum and standards committee meetings; meeting with other media specialists at local and district levels

Resources to Learn More about This Topic

One of the best resources to learn about the impact study research is the Colorado State Library's Library Research Service at <www.lrs.org>. Many impact studies are available in PDF form to download.

The Association for Supervision and Curriculum Development is a worldwide community of educators advocating sound policies and sharing best practices to achieve the success of each learner. To learn more, visit ASCD at <www.ascd.org>.

Scholastic Library Publishing. *School Libraries Work!* 26 Jan. 2007 <www.scholastic.com/librarians/printables/downloads/slw_2006.pdf>.

"Facts at a Glance…Student Achievement and the School Library Media Program" <lrs.org/documents/lmcstudies/student_achievement_2006.pdf>.

Library Research Service. *Library Impact Studies*. 26 Jan. 2007 <www.lrs.org/impact.asp>.

Pascopella, Angela. "Heart of the School: The School Library Is as Valuable as Learning How to Read and Compute. But It's a Tough Sell for Administrators." District Administration. 26 Jan. 2007 <www.districtadministration.com/page.cjm?p=960>.

Make the Connection: Quality School Library Media Programs Impact Student Achievement in Iowa by Marcia J. Rodney, Keith Curry Lance, and Christine Hamilton-Pennell at <www.aea9.k12.ia.us/download/04/aea_statewide_study.pdf> has an excellent review of the literature.

An Essential Connection: How Quality School Library Media Programs Improve Student Achievement in North Carolina by Robert Burgin and Pauletta Brown Bracy <www.rburgin.com/NCschools2003/NCSchoolStudy.pdf>.

CHAPTER FIVE

Educational and Social Science Approaches That Raise Academic Achievement

Media specialists are urged to analyze and synthesize research in disparate fields, such as education and the social sciences, that is not likely to be presented in the professional library literature. Media specialists can apply these findings and practices to their school library programs for the purpose of raising student achievement and strengthening at-risk youth. Even though this research was not designed with the library in mind, many findings are relevant. Media specialists who want to develop a school library program that impacts academic and personal achievement can learn from practitioners and researchers in these venues.

Resiliency

It is estimated that between one-half and two-thirds of children growing up in poverty and in families challenged by mental illness, alcoholism, and abusive or criminal parents are able to overcome hardships to live meaningful and productive lives (Edwards 15). The name for this ability to "bounce back successfully despite exposure to severe risks" is resiliency (Bernard 44). Mental health experts and educators have wondered why some children and teens are able to withstand great problems, while others are not. Researchers have found that resilient children have both internal and external assets that protect them from the long-term consequences of adversity and serious problems.

Let us look at Jesse, a tenth grader, who is struggling with her parents' divorce. She is not sleeping well at night and finds it impossible to concentrate in class. By evening she is too exhausted to tackle algebra problems and English essays. Her grades have slipped and she is no longer a solid B student. Her teachers have noticed changes in Jesse but none have bothered to confront her.

Unfortunately, Jesse's problem is not unique in this society. Classrooms in America are filled with students who are struggling with myriad problems such as divorce, poverty, abuse, bullying, racism, and depression that can negatively impact their education. Many times adults blame students for acting out or exhibiting unmotivated behavior without understanding the severity of the student's struggles. The findings of resiliency research provide specific guidance to adults wanting to help youth who are facing challenges.

This notion of resiliency dates back to the end of World War II. Up to that time, psychiatrists and psychologists focused on the negative outcomes of difficulties, not the possibility that individuals could recover from detrimental situations. The prevailing belief for many decades among psychologists, social workers, and counselors was that abuses, traumas, and challenges such as poverty, parental mental health, or addiction experienced early in life would derail a child forever. The research on resiliency reveals that in spite of wounds people experience, many—if not most—are able to bounce back to go on and lead healthy, productive lives. Protective factors facilitate resiliency in people's lives.

According to Nan Henderson, a social worker and co-founder of Resiliency in Action, we are hard-wired to bounce back from life's traumas, crisis, and problems. In fact, it is much more natural than not to bounce back from these things, and in the process we become wiser, more compassionate, and deeper people. Nan Henderson describes how she first learned about resiliency:

> "In the late 1980s I directed a grant for the Albuquerque Public Schools which sought to identify 'the latest in what is working in preventing and intervening with youth risk behaviors' and connect that knowledge with the emerging brain research on how kids best learn. The goal was to integrate this information into the very fabric of schools. And so in researching the latest in risk prevention, I found the concept of resiliency in Bonnie Bernard's seminal paper, *Fostering Resiliency in Youth: Protective Factors in Families, Schools, and Communities.* When I read Benard's synthesis of all the studies showing it is more likely that kids who have been labeled 'at risk' or 'high risk' will, over time, bounce back and do well in their lives, it was the most powerful epiphany of my professional life. And it resonated at a deep intuitive level. I knew I had found the answer I had been seeking about what was wrong with working from just the deficit model" [which focuses on the individual as the major problem and does not consider how the environment—parents, family, friends, school, and community— could be a significant contributor]. (Henderson email interview)

Working independently during the early 1950s, three researchers—Michael Rutter of the Institute of Psychiatry in London, Norman Garmezy of the University of Minnesota, and Emmy E. Werner of the University of California at Davis—found that a significant number of children who experienced challenges and trauma were nevertheless able to meet the developmental tasks for their age. What they uncovered flew in the face of thinking at the time. Each had exposed a new concept—a self-righting tendency of humans.

The most significant resiliency research is the Kauai Longitudinal Study which was conducted by Werner and Ruth Smith, a psychologist on the Hawaiian island of Kauai. Werner and Smith write in the introduction to *Overcoming the*

Odds: High Risk Children from Birth to Adulthood that the purpose of the study was to monitor "the impact of a variety of biological and psychosocial risk factors, stressful life events and protective factors on the development of these individuals" at birth, in infancy, early and middle childhood, late adolescence, and adulthood (1). These risk factors included chronic poverty, peri- and postnatal complications, parents with little formal education, and disorganized family environments resulting from marital discord, parental alcoholism, or parental mental illness.

Every child born on the island of Kauai in 1955 became part of this longitudinal study. Altogether, Werner and Smith followed 505 children for 40 years and discovered that certain protective factors separated the resilient children from the not-so-resilient ones. Through interviews, surveys, and assessments during the first two years of life, the research team identified children whose difficulties would most likely predict problems in late childhood and adolescence. Some of these children—42 girls and 30 boys—were designated "high risk" because they had four or more risk factors before the age of two. "Even with these factors against them, one out of three of these high-risk children developed into competent, confident, and caring young adults by age 18" (Werner and Smith *Overcoming the Odds* 2). These high-risk children who did not develop any serious learning or behavior problems in childhood or adolescence were labeled "resilient." They grew up and managed to do well in their schoolwork and in their homes and social lives.

Werner and Smith found that a cluster of three protective factors stood out as being most significant in nurturing resilience.

- The first protective cluster is at least average cognitive skills and a pleasing and sociable disposition that causes others to respond favorably to the youth
- The second protective cluster is affectionate and warm ties with adults who help the youth develop trust, autonomy, and initiative
- The third protective cluster is being able to rely on supportive organizations such as churches, youth groups, or schools
- Many resilient children also remembered a supportive and encouraging teacher

In addition, Werner and Smith found that resilient youth had developed good reading and reasoning skills in grade school, a positive attitude toward education, set realistic vocational plans in high school, and had a hobby or interest that their peers respected. In *Journeys from Childhood to Midlife: Risk, Resilience, and Recovery*, Werner and Smith write that "nowhere were the differences between the resilient individuals and their peers with problems in adolescence more apparent than in the goals they had set for themselves for their adult lives." Resilient youth had faith that one's own life could be shaped by their actions taken and "odds can be surmounted." Resilient youth were more likely to participate in extracurricular activities such as 4-H, YMCA, and YWCA. Most important, resilient children had established a close bond with at least one caretaker. They found emotional support outside the family in a "teacher who had become a role model, friend, or confident"

(57). Although Werner and Smith did not set out to prove that media specialists strengthen youth, it is nevertheless true that school library programs naturally incorporate many protective factors identified in the Kauai Longitudinal Study.

Research in the 1960s which focused on making the connection between stressful life events and illness found that "some individuals are more susceptible or vulnerable than others, due both to physiological and psychological differences (either inborn or acquired very early), and to the degree of prior success they have enjoyed (or not) in coping with life experiences. Furthermore, there may well be vulnerable periods of life when difficult experiences are more likely than during other times to overwhelm the individual" (Haggerty, et al. xvi). Media specialists who grasp this previous quote will appreciate individual differences, base programs and services on the protective factors that build individual strengths, offer opportunities to experience success, and recognize the vulnerability of childhood and adolescence. The message of resiliency is not to give up on the students we know because most will succeed when protective factors are put into place.

Henderson writes about the importance of "surrounding each person— as well as families and organizations—with all elements of 'The Resiliency Wheel'" (10). Based on the resiliency findings, Henderson's wheel is a graphical representation that leads to understanding what to do to build up the environment while at the same time lessening environmental risk factors. Figure 5.1 identifies factors needed in an environment that strengthens youth, as well as factors that could lessen the impact of environments that are less than optimal.

Figure 5.1 *The Resiliency Wheel*

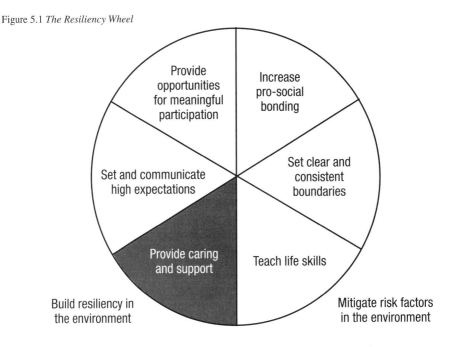

Source: Nan Henderson and Resiliency in Action at <www.resiliency.com>. Reprinted by Permission.

The first strategy is to *add* protective factors to the environment. Youth are strengthened by caring and supportive relationships, high expectations, and opportunities for meaningful participation. The most important of these is to provide caring and support. "Providing oneself and others with unconditional positive regard, love, and encouragement is the most powerful external resiliency-builder" (Henderson 10). The question media specialists should ask is: "How can I nurture and support students?"

Henderson writes about how one school set high, but realistic expectations for success: "One middle school I worked with changed its 'Honor Roll' program to an 'On a Roll' program. In order to be recognized as 'On a Roll' students need only raise their grades one letter" (10). An important way to help students deal with their own problems and struggles is—paradoxically—to encourage them to help others.

The second strategy is to *lessen* the risk factors in the environment. This is accomplished by increasing prosocial bonding, setting clear and consistent boundaries, and teaching life skills. Henderson writes, "people who are positively bonded to other people (through a network of friends and family and/or clubs or organizations) and to enjoyable activities do better in life" (11).

How can media specialists encourage prosocial bonding? Media specialists promote social skills when they support and host activities that encourage students to collaborate together and make friends. An example of one such program is "The Lunch Bunch," developed by Nelle Martin, a high school media specialist in Florida. When Martin noticed that the same students came alone to the school library every day during lunch instead of spending time with friends in the cafeteria, she talked to them and learned that most were new to the school and had not yet made friends. To help them with this transition, Martin let these students eat lunch together in an out-of-the-way spot in the school library. She purchased games for them to play during lunch. Sometimes "The Lunch Bunch" students helped Martin by performing minor chores around the media center. Martin was truly astounded to see how these students flourished as they developed friendships within the group and connected to the school through the library. The informal program Martin established can easily be replicated in other schools by media specialists who recognize the importance of helping youth develop social skills, make friends, and establish connections. This program won Martin the Florida Association for Media in Education's (FAME) first Amanda Award in 2002. The Amanda Award recognizes media specialists who develop programs that strengthen and develop the self-esteem of students.

Think About...

Are there programs in your school library that are specifically designed to strengthen at-risk students? Are there others that you believe have the kinds of characteristics or impact students in the ways described in the previous examples?

A final way to build resiliency is to teach life skills, such as good communication and listening skills, healthy conflict resolution, and assertiveness. At one time Henderson worked in an adolescent drug treatment center. When she asked one drug-abusing adolescent how he ended up in treatment, he replied: "I got to middle school and felt lost. I didn't have any friends. I didn't know how to navigate in this big, strange, impersonal place. So, I did the only thing I saw to do. I went out behind the gym and joined the group there lighting up and drinking" (11). Helping students develop the life skills to enter and participate in schools, make friends, and feel confidence in themselves becomes more critical as students transition to the increasingly bigger and more complex environments of middle and high school.

No discussion about resiliency would be complete without mentioning the contributions of Bonnie Benard. For over 25 years, Benard has helped children and youth live healthier, drug-free lives. She develops resources, provides training and professional development, and presents to national and international audiences best practices in the field of prevention and resilience/youth development theory and policy. By synthesizing resiliency research, Benard has brought these findings to educators and other practitioners.

Benard's work has directly affected national policy. Title IV (Safe and Drug-Free Schools and Communities) of the federal *No Child Left Behind Act* requires that school districts across the country now consider resilience factors such as caring adults in their school along with risk factors (e.g., bullying and harassment at school) in their school assessments. This major change in policy was a direct result of Benard's 15 years of promoting resilience and the connection between social and emotional development and learning. Because of her work, schools and districts in California are monitoring whether they are providing the critical development supports and opportunities that promote healthy development and learning.

Marzano and Translating Research into Action

A second framework for improving academic achievement is Robert J. Marzano's book *What Works in Schools: Translating Research into Action*, which is a synthesis of research regarding the general factors that influence student achievement. According to Marzano, "if we follow the guidance offered from 35 years of research, we can enter an era of unprecedented effectiveness for the public practice of education—one in which the vast majority of schools can be highly effective in promoting student learning" (1). Marzano organizes the research findings into three categories:

- School-level factors
- Teacher-level factors
- Student-level factors

"We know what works in education. The research is prolific. The question today is not what works or what does not work. Rather it is why is it that we know what constitutes good teaching and effective learning and yet we fail to implement what we know" (16).

School-Level Factors

The school-level factors that research has shown improve academic achievement are:

- *Guaranteed and viable curriculum*
- *Challenging goals and effective feedback*
- *Parent and community involvement*
- *Safe and orderly environment*
- *Collegiality and professionalism*

Guaranteed and Viable Curriculum

Marzano describes this as one in which students have the "opportunity to learn," which comes down to whether or not students have been taught the subject matter. Often students attending low-SES schools do not have the same opportunities as students attending higher-SES schools to take rigorous courses that are college preparatory. Nell Duke of Michigan State University compared literacy opportunities of first-grade students attending either high- or low-SES schools and found major differences between the two. She writes, "literacy is another domain through which schools may contribute to lower levels of achievement among low-SES children and may begin to do so quite early in the schooling process" (Duke 441).

Because it is so imperative that students have time to learn the subject matter, the instructional time must be protected from unnecessary disruptions, socializing, informal breaks, and other activities that do not lead to student learning. Marzano recommends that teachers understand what is considered essential to teach, ensure that the essential content can be addressed in the amount of time available for instruction, and organize and sequence the essential content so students have ample time to learn it.

Challenging Goals and Effective Feedback

In addition to opportunity to learn, students benefit from high expectations and having their progress monitored and communicated to them. Students in classes where clear learning goals were communicated experienced a 21 percentage point difference in achievement (Marzano 35). Edwards, a leader of the school effectiveness movement of the 1970s, believes that "high expectations for students, particularly those from low-SES backgrounds, are a cornerstone of the school effectiveness research" (36). In addition, according to Marzano's synthesis of research, the impact setting goals has on student achievement can range from a low of 18 percentile points to a high of 41 percentile points (35). In order to understand exactly what their weaknesses and strengths are, students need regular feedback that is timely and content specific rather than a broad assessment. The media specialist can collaborate with teachers to present joint lessons and access and evaluate the information components.

Parent and Community Involvement

Marzano defines this as a process of communication, participation, and governance (47). However, it is the responsibility of schools—not parents—to foster two-way communication. The onus is on schools to establish vehicles of communication and to find ways for parents to be involved in the day-to-day running of the school. Likewise, this is such an important responsibility of the media specialist that it is a component of Standard X, Library Media/Early Childhood through Young Adulthood, of the National Board of Professional Teaching Standards (NBPTS): "Accomplished library media specialists understand that active, involved, and informed families create a network that supports vital opportunities for learning."

Safe and Orderly Environment

In a 1997 study on the effect of violence on student achievement, Grogger (in Marzano 54) found that math scores were .20 of a standard deviation lower and students were 5.7 percent less likely to graduate in schools with a high incidence of violence. Action steps to build a safe and orderly environment include:

- Creating rules and procedures for behavioral problems and for general behavior
- Establishing positive consequences for following rules as well as appropriate consequences for violations of rules and procedures
- Teaching students how to monitor and discipline themselves

Think About...
Which school library rules and procedures or programs add to students' feelings of safety?

Collegiality and Professionalism

Defined as support teachers provide one another, collegiality and professionalism is characterized by authentic interactions such as openly sharing failures and mistakes, demonstrating respect for one another, and constructively analyzing and criticizing practices and procedures. Even though many schools encourage social interactions as a way to build collegiality, there is a negative correlation between student achievement and "friendship" interactions among teachers. Furthermore, Marzano reports that the higher the number of friendship interactions, the lower the students' academic achievement (61).

Teacher-Level Factors

The teacher-level factors that research has shown improve academic achievement are:

- *Instructional strategies*
- *Classroom management*
- *Classroom and curriculum design*

Instructional Strategies

Effective teachers use effective instructional strategies. Examples of proven effective strategies are: use of experiments and inquiry-based learning; classroom time management; direct instruction; memorization; questioning; homework; classroom assessment; advanced organizers; feedback; mastery learning; ability grouping and clarity of presentation.

Other instructional strategies that are particularly effective are identifying similarities and differences, summarizing, note taking and tutoring (79).

Classroom Management

This entails establishing and enforcing rules and procedures, carrying out disciplinary actions, developing good teacher and student relationships, and maintaining an appropriate mental set which includes "withitness" and emotional objectivity.

"Withitness" is an educational term coined by Jacob Kounin who conducted two research studies in the 1970s on the topic of classroom management that refers to a teacher's awareness of what is occurring in the classroom. Kounin found that effective teachers handle discipline problems similarly to ineffective teachers, but what differentiated the two is that the former were able to prevent misbehavior before it occurred. One quality that effective teachers have is "withitness," which is described as having "eyes in the back of one's head."

Can Do...

Visit the School Discipline site at <teacherpathfinder.org/Support/discipline.html> and match up your school library's rules and your disciplinary practices with the ones mentioned on the site.

Classroom and Curriculum Design

Marzano identifies two principles that lead to improved academic achievement: One, learning is enhanced when a teacher identifies specific types of knowledge that are the focus of a unit or lesson; two, learning requires engagement in tasks that are structured or are sufficiently similar to allow for effective transfer of knowledge. He makes the point that when "students are first exposed to content, learning should ideally involve the use of stories or other forms of dramatization along with the use of visual representations of information. In subsequent exposures, learning experiences should involve discussion and (ideally) tasks that require students to make and defend judgments" (114).

Can Do...

Match picture books, story books, and high-interest-low-readability texts with curricular units. Label each book's spine and note this information in the MARC record so teachers can search for these materials in the catalog.

Student-Level Factors

In addition to school-level and teacher-level factors that improve academic achievement, there are three student-level factors that improve academic achievement. These are:

- *Home environment*
- *Learned intelligence*
- *Background knowledge of students*

Home Environment

Even though socioeconomic status (SES) is a predictor of academic achievement, it is too simplistic to view low-SES families as unable to further their children's academic success. In a meta-analysis of 101 reports, Karl White (Marzano 127) found that the following four elements of SES have the most effect on student achievement:

- Income of parents or adults in the home
- Education of adults in the home
- Occupation of adults in the home
- The atmosphere in the home

It is the home atmosphere that has the strongest impact on student achievement. White explains, "It is not at all implausible that some low-SES parents (defined in terms of income, education, and/or occupational level) are very good at creating a home atmosphere that fosters learning (e.g., read to their children, help them with their homework, encourage them to go to college, and take them to the library and to cultural events), whereas other low-SES parents are not" (127). Action steps include:

- Encouraging parents to communicate with their children about school
- Teaching parents to monitor and supervise their child's after-school activities and homework
- Encouraging effective parenting styles

Learned Intelligence and Background Knowledge

Engaging in activities aimed at enhancing the background knowledge of students produced increased academic achievement. Background knowledge can be increased through field trips to cultural activities, by establishing mentoring opportunities so the student has the opportunity to engage in a steady and trusting relationship with a caring and successful adult, and through vocabulary development.

Vocabulary development is instrumental to reading, but some approaches are more beneficial than others. Marzano writes that wide reading—also called free voluntary reading—"as the sole vehicle for vocabulary development" is not the best approach (139). "Whereas wide reading certainly is critical to vocabulary development, research over the decades simply does not support the position that it is sufficient in and of itself to ensure proper vocabulary development" (139). Wide reading with vocabulary instruction must focus on identifying interesting words, talking about their meaning, and encouraging students to keep track of their words in a personal vocabulary notebook. Students benefit by elaborating on and discussing the meaning of new words or by generating imagery or visual representations of the meaning of words (140).

Student Motivation

The link between student motivation and achievement is very strong. Marzano provides four action steps to awaken motivation in students.

- Provide students with feedback on their individual growth
- Provide students with tasks and activities that are engaging and interesting
- Provide opportunities for students to construct and work on long-term projects of their own design
- Teach students about the dynamics of motivation (149-152)

These research-based strategies and practices will be fully applied to the media center in the following section. Marzano writes that efforts to improve student achievement will look different from school to school; the emphasis is on effective instructional practices that are proven through research designs; change is slow and occurs incrementally; and leadership is the single most important aspect of school reform (158-159).

The National Dropout Prevention Center/ Network Guidelines

The National Dropout Prevention Center/Network (NDPC/N), located at Clemson University in South Carolina, serves "as a research center and resource network for practitioners, researchers, and policymakers to reshape school and community environments to meet the needs of youth in at-risk situations so these students receive the quality education and services necessary to succeed academically and graduate from high school." In addition to dropout prevention, a second focus of this organization is on preventing dropout of students with disabilities, as discussed in Chapter Two. Following is a list of the strategies and explanatory information. For additional information about each of these strategies, as well as model programs, access the NDPC/N Web site at <www.dropoutprevention.org/>. Information in this chapter is based on the NDPC/N Web site and is used with their permission.

By synthesizing and analyzing research, the NDPC/N has identified 15 strategies for dropout prevention in the following four categories: school and community perspective; early interventions; basic core strategies; and making the most of instruction.

School and community perspective includes the following three strategies:

1. *Systemic Renewal.* This is a continuing process to improve education by evaluating goals and objectives related to school policies, current instructional practices, and organizational structures as they impact a diverse group of learners.
2. *School and Community Collaboration.* Education is a community effort—not just the responsibility of schools. When all groups in a community provide collective support to the school, a strong infrastructure sustains a caring supportive environment where youth can thrive and achieve.
3. *Safe Learning Environments.* A study conducted in the mid-1990s by the Educational Development Center found that only half of all children felt safe in school and approximately 160,000 students per day miss school because they fear physical harm. A safe learning environment provides daily experiences, at all grade levels, that enhance positive social attitudes and effective interpersonal skills in all students.

Early interventions include the following three strategies:

1. *Family Engagement.* Research consistently finds that family engagement has a direct, positive effect on children's achievement and is the most accurate predictor of a student's success in school. Schargel and Smink (2001) write that the most accurate predictor of a student's achievement in school is not income or social status, but the extent to which their family is able to (a) create a home environment that encourages learning; (b) communicate high, yet reasonable, expectations for their children's achievement and future careers; and (c) become involved in their children's education at school and in the community.

   According to the National Parent Teacher Association, when parents are involved, students achieve more, regardless of socioeconomic status, ethnic/racial background, or the parents' education level. These students have higher grades and test scores, better attendance, and complete homework more consistently. Likewise, they have higher graduation rates and greater enrollment rates in postsecondary education.

2. *Early Childhood Education.* Birth-to-five interventions demonstrate that providing a child additional enrichment can enhance brain development. The most effective way to reduce the number of children who will ultimately drop out is to provide the best possible classroom instruction from the beginning of their school experience through the primary grades.

Think About...

How can the media specialist develop background knowledge and provide enriching experiences for students in the primary grades?

3. *Early Childhood Literacy.* Early interventions to help low-achieving students improve their reading and writing skills establish the necessary foundation for effective learning in all other subjects. The NDPC/N reports the following statistics about literacy: more than half of all fourth graders who are eligible for the free lunch program fail to read at the basic achievement level needed for academic success; 68% of fourth graders in the highest-poverty public schools fail to reach the basic level of achievement and only one in ten reads at the proficient level; low literacy levels show a strong correlation with poverty, crime and unemployment; on average, welfare recipients ages 17 to 21 read at the sixth-grade level; and 70% of prisoners read in the two lowest levels of reading proficiency.

Basic Core Strategies include the following four strategies:

1. *Mentoring.* This is a one-to-one caring, supportive relationship between a mentor and a mentee that is based on trust. The mentor is simply a wise and trusted friend with a commitment to provide guidance and support so the mentee can develop to their fullest potential based on their vision for the future. Mentoring can occur in a traditional one-to-one relationship, a one-to-group relationship, or on the Internet. This latter form of mentoring is called telementoring.

2. *Service Learning.* This is a powerful learning and teaching method that connects meaningful community service experiences with academic learning, personal growth, and civic responsibility. There are many reasons why students drop out of school, but the most common ones are boredom and disaffection. Service-learning is an active learning strategy that connects students to the school and the real world.

3. *Alternative Schooling.* Many times students who are failing in a traditional educational setting will succeed in an alternative one. Alternative Schooling programs pay special attention to the struggling student's individual social needs and academic requirements for a high school diploma.

4. *After-School Opportunities.* Many schools provide after-school and summer enhancement programs that eliminate information loss and inspire interest in a variety of areas. Such experiences are especially important for students at risk of school failure because these programs fill the afternoon gap time with constructive and engaging activities. Many disadvantaged students in urban and rural environments lack the day-to-day experiences that stimulate their intellectual development. After-school opportunities have positive effects on academic success, social behavior, and provide opportunities for enrichment for at-risk students.

The final category, ***Making the Most of Instruction***, includes the following five strategies and practices:

1. *Professional Development.* Teachers who work with youth at high risk of academic failure need to feel supported and have an avenue by which they can continue to develop skills, techniques, and learn about innovative strategies. A study by Haycock that is fully cited on the NDPC/N Web site discovered that low-achieving students increased their achievement level by as much as 53 percent when taught by a highly effective teacher.

2. *Active Learning.* This is a general term for teaching and learning strategies that engage and involve students in the learning process. Research has shown that not everyone learns in the same way. Some of us are visual learners that need to see to understand, while others need to hear or verbalize information. Others are hands-on, kinesthetic

learners. Some learners prefer to work alone, while some like to teach each other in small groups. Some need time to quietly reflect, while others need to move and be active. Teachers know that they need to use a variety of activities to meet the learning styles of their students.

At-risk students often struggle to learn in a traditional classroom. Classrooms where learning activities are varied give these students the opportunity to excel. Students become involved in their learning rather than disinterested. Involved learners enjoy school and become lifelong learners.

Can Do...

Identify three strategies you will implement to strengthen youth based on these findings.

3. *Educational Technology*. Technology offers some of the best opportunities for engaging students in authentic learning, addressing multiple intelligences, and adapting to students' learning styles. A February 2000 report by the National Center for Education Statistics states that even though 95 percent of all public schools were connected to the Internet by 1999, merely providing connectivity is not enough. There must be qualified teachers to use the technology and teach students how to use it. The need for qualified teachers is particularly acute in Title I schools. In addition, there is concern over the growing digital divide between low-income and middle-class families and schools. Research conducted by Irving found that households earning more than $75,000 are more than 20 times more likely to have home Internet access than those at the lowest income levels.

4. *Individualized Instruction*. Each student has unique interests and past learning experiences. An individualized instructional program provides flexibility in teaching methods and motivational strategies to target individual differences. The best way to understand individualized instruction is to look at how it is used in special education. The Individualized Education Program (IEP) provides the foundation for learning and is developed as a collaborative effort of students (when appropriate), teachers, parents, school administrators, and related services personnel. Many schools are now using IEPs with students who score below grade level on standardized tests. Unfortunately, most regular teachers do not have the time to provide IEPs for all of their students.

The most effective way to learn something for the first time is to connect it to prior knowledge. To do this, teachers must first know (using pre-testing, questioning, and observation) each child's knowledge level. The next step is to use a constructivist educational approach to help students give meaning to new learning based on their prior knowledge. Active, experiential learning is vital to the construction of new knowledge. Some of the instructional strategies that encourage knowledge building are:

- Problem-based learning and reciprocal teaching
- Peer tutoring
- Cooperative learning
- Hands-on learning
- Journaling
- Projects
- Role play
- Simulation
- Inquiry

5. *Career and Technology Education.* A quality Career and Technology Education program and a related guidance program are essential for all students. School-to-work programs recognize that youth need specific skills to prepare them to measure up to the larger demands of today's workplace.

Resources to Learn More about These Topics

Books

Bernard, Bonnie. *Fostering Resiliency in Kids: Protective Factors in Families, Schools, and Communities.* 26 Jan. 2007 <nwrac.org/pub/library/f/f_foster.pdf>.

Benard, Bonnie. *Resiliency: What We Have Learned.* San Francisco: WestEd, 2004.

Doll, Beth, Steven Zucker, and Katherine Brehm. *Resiliency Classrooms: Creating Healthy Environments for Learning.* New York: Guildford, 2004.

Henderson, Nan, Bonnie Benard, and Nancy Sharp-Light, eds. *Resiliency In Action: Practical Ideas for Overcoming Risks and Building Strengths.* Ojai: Resiliency In Action, 2007.

Henderson, Nan, and Mike M. Milstein. *Resiliency in Schools: Making it Happen for Students and Educators.* Thousand Oaks: Corwin, 2003.

Jones, Jami L. *Bouncing Back: Dealing with the Stuff Life Throws at You.* New York: Franklin Watts, 2007.

Krovetz, Martin L. *Fostering Resiliency: Expecting All Students to Use Their Minds and Hearts Well.* Thousand Oaks: Corwin, 1999.

Milstein, Mike M., and Doris Annie Henry. *Spreading Resiliency: Making it Happen for Schools and Communities.* Thousand Oaks: Corwin, 2000.

Sykes, Judith Anne. *Brain Friendly School Libraries.* Westport: Libraries Unlimited, 2006.

Web Sites

To read about the important role of communication and the school library program, go to the NBPTS Web site at <www.nbpts.org> and click on the tab for Candidates, then select Library Media from the pull-down menu.

More information about the Amanda Award is available at FAME's Web site at <www.floridamedia.org/awards/awards.html>.

SECTION THREE

Applying What Works to the School Library

Introduction

The focus of Section Three is to develop a school library program that improves academic achievement and strengthens at-risk youth. The framework used to do this is resiliency and the vehicles for doing this are the *Resiliency Wheel* and the *Library Ladder of Resiliency*. In Chapter Six, the *Resiliency Wheel* and the *Library Ladder of Resiliency* will be used to create a turnaround, or holistic, library that nurtures the social, academic, and spiritual needs of students and improves academic achievement.

It is a concept that is gaining recognition. The Association for Supervision and Curriculum Development has established a campaign called the *Whole Child* for the purpose of ensuring that children are healthy, safe, engaged, supported, and challenged and their "unique capacities for intellectual, social, emotional, physical, and spiritual learning" are restored (ASCD 2). School libraries whose goals and objectives are based on the resiliency model are natural partners to participate in this effort to improve academic achievement by creating the "learning conditions that enable all children to develop all of their gifts and realize their fullest potential" (2). In Chapter Seven, readers will learn to implement change using the systems change model and to evaluate their turnaround school library program to determine whether it does in fact improve student achievement and strengthen at-risk youth.

What Are Dispositions?

Webster's dictionary defines *dispositions* as "the natural mental and emotional outlook or mood; it is a characteristic attitude. Dispositions represent the prevailing personal beliefs as shown in behavior and in relationships with others." Increasingly, national and state teacher accreditation bodies include dispositions in their standards for professionals.

Dispositions are not new to professionalism. Every human service role has a code of ethics and a standard for behavior. The increasing attention to the characteristics and behaviors of education professionals is based on the recognition that those who are most successful with students, particularly students who are at risk, model high standards.

It is important to recognize that dispositions do not encompass personality styles. Media specialists are not required to be perky or quiet and formal. They are, however, required to exhibit professional demeanor and commitment, and bring these qualities to bear in their interactions with students and colleagues.

David C. Whaley, in his research on how one state, Colorado, assessed dispositions, indicates that they include both personal characteristics such as initiative and critical thinking, and contextual characteristics such as a desire to continuously develop as a professional. Dispositions represent the professionalism and commitment that research indicates is necessary to engage in practices that effectively help all students succeed. During the 2003-2004 academic year, the Council of Teacher Education at East Carolina University created a survey to assess dispositions of teacher education candidates in three categories: demeanor, commitment, and interactions. Likewise, the Arkansas Department of Education has identified the following dispositions for its teachers:

- The teacher believes that all children can learn at high levels and persists in helping all children achieve success
- The teacher is willing to respond with different approaches until the student succeeds
- The teacher is committed to lifelong learning
- The teacher is willing to explore and use technologies in the classroom (NCATE)

Similarly, there are dispositions in librarianship. Dr. Elizabeth Haynes of the University of Southern Mississippi has identified the dispositions that are embedded in the American Association of School Librarians (a division of the American Library Association)/National Council for Accreditation of Teacher Education (NCATE) standards for school media specialists. These include: enjoys reading; works well with others; advocates for flexible access; and is collaborative. In another ALA division, the Young Adult Library Services Association, dispositions for youth workers are identified. These include: leadership and professionalism; knowledge of client group; communication; administration; knowledge of materials; access to information; and services.

The research presented in Chapter Four paints a clear picture that effective school library programs do impact the academic achievement of students; however, other than finding that it is important to have a credentialed and professional media specialist at the helm, particular dispositions or personality traits were not identified.

Are there dispositions and traits that effective media specialists exhibit? In this relatively untapped area of research, two recent studies may provide some answers. In the first instance of research, a study recently conducted but yet unpublished by Jami Biles Jones and Rejeanor Scott, supervisor of media for the Pitt County School District in Greenville, North Carolina, found that media specialists who completed the NEO-Five Factor Inventory that measures the five personality traits of neuroticism, conscientiousness, extraversion, agreeableness, and openness to new experiences scored higher on the latter three traits than the control group used to develop this well-respected inventory. Individuals who are agreeable are friendly, cooperative, and trusting. Individuals who are open to new experiences are imaginative and original. Individuals high in extraversion tend to be energetic and enthusiastic. The second study was conducted by researchers at North Carolina State University (NCSU) to determine the "transformational" leadership styles (Kouzes and Posner) of the principal, media specialist, and technology facilitator at ten schools in North Carolina that received grants to implement IMPACT, which is a model for infusing technology into teaching and learning. The five "transformational" leadership practices defined by James M. Kouzes and Barry Z. Posner are: challenging the process; inspiring a shared vision; enabling others to act; modeling the way; and encouraging the heart. Media specialists were rated highest in the area of enabling others to act, which seems reasonable considering the instrumental role they assume as the "primary conduits of resources" (Bradburn and Osborn).

Impact study research indicates that effective school libraries have a professional and credentialed media specialist at their helm. However, educational degrees and credentials do not necessarily equate to effectiveness. One can deduce that effective school librarians share certain dispositions, traits, or characteristics that research is beginning to identify.

CHAPTER SIX

The Turnaround School Library

Students thrive academically when instructional practices are effective; likewise, they are strengthened when the environment in which they learn is nurturing and supportive. Werner and Smith found in their research that resilient youth often remembered a special teacher who had "become a role model, friend, and confidant for them" (57). The compelling reason for focusing on the affective needs of students is that many who are not achieving in schools and are the focus of *No Child Left Behind* face multiple challenges such as poverty, discrimination, and a language barrier that may stand in the way of learning. These challenges cannot be overcome solely by improving instructional practices; rather, the whole child must be strengthened. Building resiliency is one way to address academic failure by boosting feelings of well-being and connectedness to others who care.

Interestingly, reading, perhaps the biggest academic shortcoming faced by students, can be improved through mentoring, which is the most significant protective factor identified in the resiliency research conducted by Werner and Smith. In order for children to become literate they must have the vocabulary to understand ideas, concepts, and experiences, but many students who are the focus of this book come to school without the background knowledge to support vocabulary development. Even the most carefully chosen collection is not going to improve this situation, but a proactive media specialist who understands how to build background knowledge can.

Although the best way to increase background knowledge, and thereby develop vocabulary and improve reading, is to increase out-of-class experiences through travel and field trips to museums and art galleries, this can be expensive. But media specialists can use their knowledge of technology and resources to provide students with inexpensive virtual trips and experiences. However, two other ways to build a student's background knowledge are affordable and together provide an opportunity for the media specialist to improve reading scores while increasing a student's connectedness to school.

The first way to develop background knowledge is through mentoring, which is a one-to-one relationship between a caring adult and youth who needs support. Mentoring is central to building an environment that helps students achieve. Mentoring exposes children to new ideas and concepts, and to people they can talk to and learn from.

A second way to develop background knowledge is through vocabulary development. Chomsky (Marzano *Direct* 52) was one of the first linguists to provide a compelling argument that language and thought are inextricably linked. Simply, vocabulary is the building block of thought: "Without knowledge of the vocabulary terms that describe an experience, an individual has no way to express the experience semantically" (53). This is why vocabulary development is so important to reading. Media specialists can help students increase vocabulary skills by focusing efforts on helping students learn words and phrases that are critical to understanding curricular content. Students should be exposed to new words multiple times—preferably about six times. Have students represent their understanding of new words using mental images, such as pictures and symbols. Have students summarize a story by drawing the scenes. The goal is not necessarily an in-depth understanding of new words, but to provide students with an accurate, surface knowledge and recognition of new words to help them understand content. This example of reading shows that effective instruction coupled with meeting the affective and holistic needs of students improves academic achievement. For many students, an emphasis on academic achievement without meeting their holistic needs does not lead to satisfactory improvement.

Think About...

Booktalks are a fun way to pique children's interest in reading but you may want to rethink how yours is organized. Instead of presenting books by author or theme, focus on developing background experiences or teaching vocabulary words that support what is being taught in the classroom.

Figure 6.1 Profile of a Student Needing Resiliency Improvement

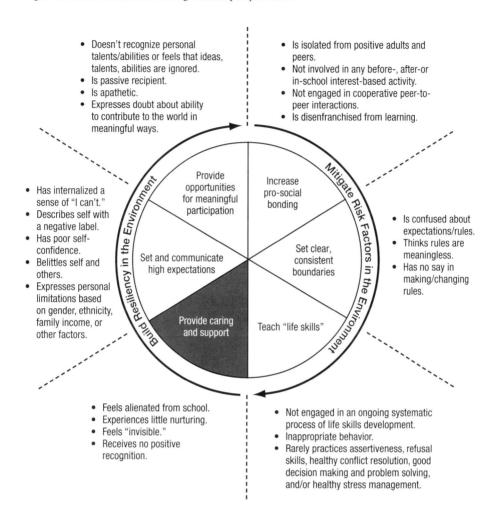

• Doesn't recognize personal talents/abilities or feels that ideas, talents, abilities are ignored.
• Is passive recipient.
• Is apathetic.
• Expresses doubt about ability to contribute to the world in meaningful ways.

• Is isolated from positive adults and peers.
• Not involved in any before-, after-or in-school interest-based activity.
• Not engaged in cooperative peer-to-peer interactions.
• Is disenfranchised from learning.

• Has internalized a sense of "I can't."
• Describes self with a negative label.
• Has poor self-confidence.
• Belittles self and others.
• Expresses personal limitations based on gender, ethnicity, family income, or other factors.

• Is confused about expectations/rules.
• Thinks rules are meaningless.
• Has no say in making/changing rules.

• Feels alienated from school.
• Experiences little nurturing.
• Feels "invisible."
• Receives no positive recognition.

• Not engaged in an ongoing systematic process of life skills development.
• Inappropriate behavior.
• Rarely practices assertiveness, refusal skills, healthy conflict resolution, good decision making and problem solving, and/or healthy stress management.

Source: Henderson, Nan, and Mike M. Milstein. *Resiliency in Schools: Making It Happen for Students and Educators* p. 21, copyright 2003 by Corwin Press. Reprinted by Permission of Corwin Press Inc.

As discussed in Section One, the high school dropout rate which hovers around 30% indicates that many students are not being well served by the American educational system. It is unfair to blame students for failing without pointing a finger at schools and recognizing the organizational barriers within schools that stand in the way of embracing the resiliency-promoting strategies that students need to be successful. The barriers to student performance have little to do with them, but rather the perceptions of teachers and the school environment. Several of these barriers are: perceived time limitations; the controversy over the role of school in the lives of students; the large size of schools; and "the absence of specific resiliency-fostering teaching strategies, school and classroom organization, and programs of prevention and intervention" (Henderson and Milstein 19-20). Schools characterized by these barriers are more likely to have students similar to those identified in Figure 6.1 on page 69. Henderson and Milstein believe that "this passion for helping students to be resilient, coupled with knowledge from the resiliency literature about how to do it, is the driving force behind overcoming barriers to resiliency building" (21). This passion stems from dispositions and personality traits but can be developed by conscientious media specialists who are open to new paradigms such as creating an environment in which students thrive. The turnaround or holistic school library is the new paradigm.

Think About...

Which students do you know fit the profile of a student needing resiliency improvement? How can you strengthen them?

Media specialists can counteract barriers to academic achievement and promote strength in students by implementing a school library program based on the six resiliency elements shown in the *Resiliency Wheel* in Chapter Five. Students who are experiencing adversity and challenge need to be immersed in an environment that provides protective factors that buffer difficulties because "with enough 'protection,' the individual adapts to that adversity without experiencing a significant disruption in his or her life" (Henderson and Milstein 5). Often, these disruptions translate into missing classes, not being able to concentrate on school work, and loss of motivation, which can lead to academic failure.

There are six elements to fostering resiliency:

1. **Increase pro-social bonding** by connecting students with their peers and adults and activities that build friendships and connections. Children with strong positive bonds are less likely to become involved in risky behaviors that could jeopardize their future such as drugs and early unwanted pregnancies.
2. **Set clear and consistent boundaries** so youth understand what is expected of them. Procedures and policies that are clearly written and communicated are more likely to result in appropriate consequences that are consistently enforced.
3. **Teach "life skills"** such as cooperation, healthy conflict resolution, resistance and assertiveness skills, communication skills, problem-solving and decision-making skills, and healthy stress management. Students who are taught life skills and internalize these teachings are more likely to resist risky situations that could lead to academic failure.

4. **Provide caring and support** is the most critical of these six elements because "it seems almost impossible to successfully 'overcome' adversity without the presence of caring" (Henderson and Milstein 13). Educational reformers recognize that the foundation for academic success is an environment in which care and support is communicated.
5. **Set and communicate high expectations** that are realistic so that students may utilize their abilities to reach their potentials. These expectations need to be high but realistic.
6. **Provide opportunities for meaningful participation** so students can practice life skills in a nurturing environment that accepts and communicates the notion that practice makes perfect and does not penalize students for missing the mark.

A useful way to understand how to implement the six elements of the *Resiliency Wheel* in a school library is by creating a scenario developed for this purpose. The following describes Mrs. McCormick and how she created a school library program at Johnson Middle School that addresses academic failure by implanting instructional strategies, as well as strengthening students.

THE SCENARIO

Mrs. McCormick has been a media specialist for six years, but this is her second year at Johnson Middle School. Mrs. McCormick has noticed that students seem apathetic and disinterested, but she has three definite concerns about students at Johnson Middle School that she wants to address.

1. Many students enter middle school and begin to fail even though they earned excellent grades in elementary school.
2. For many students, reading in middle school slackens and tapers off even though they were avid readers in elementary school.
3. Many students do not possess skills to manage school stressors and are not prepared to make decisions about their future that must be made in high school.

To address these concerns, Mrs. McCormick decides to organize the school library program so that it addresses academic failure, reading, and life skills by strengthening the individual. After reading the book *Resiliency in Schools: Making it Happen for Students and Educators* by Nan Henderson and Mike M. Milstein, she believes that caring relationships and a nurturing environment are the foundation for academic achievement. Therefore, she decides that relationships with students are more important than shelving books, completing a book order, or any other library task (although these must be done). Her objective is to create an environment that nurtures students to become resilient as profiled in Figure 6.2. At the end of the school year, Mrs. McCormick will compare circulation statistics, grade point averages, and attendance at school library events with previous years numbers and hold focus groups with students and faculty to determine whether the turnaround school library impacts grades, reading, and the development and utilization of life skills. With that goal in mind she applies the six elements of the *Resiliency Wheel* to the Johnson Middle School library.

Figure 6.2 Profile of a Student with Characteristics of Resiliency

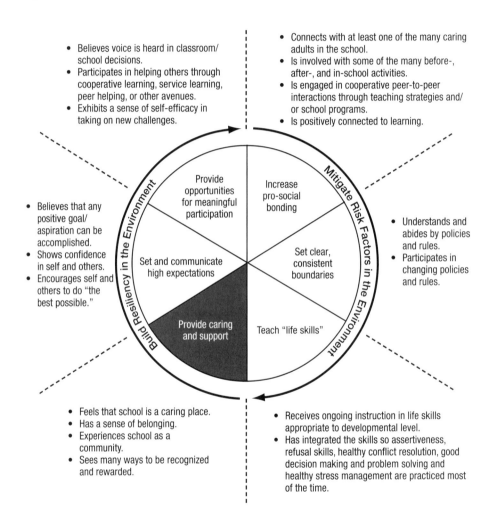

- Believes voice is heard in classroom/school decisions.
- Participates in helping others through cooperative learning, service learning, peer helping, or other avenues.
- Exhibits a sense of self-efficacy in taking on new challenges.

- Connects with at least one of the many caring adults in the school.
- Is involved with some of the many before-, after-, and in-school activities.
- Is engaged in cooperative peer-to-peer interactions through teaching strategies and/or school programs.
- Is positively connected to learning.

- Believes that any positive goal/aspiration can be accomplished.
- Shows confidence in self and others.
- Encourages self and others to do "the best possible."

- Understands and abides by policies and rules.
- Participates in changing policies and rules.

- Feels that school is a caring place.
- Has a sense of belonging.
- Experiences school as a community.
- Sees many ways to be recognized and rewarded.

- Receives ongoing instruction in life skills appropriate to developmental level.
- Has integrated the skills so assertiveness, refusal skills, healthy conflict resolution, good decision making and problem solving and healthy stress management are practiced most of the time.

Wheel labels: Build Resiliency in the Environment; Mitigate Risk Factors in the Environment; Provide opportunities for meaningful participation; Increase pro-social bonding; Set and communicate high expectations; Set clear, consistent boundaries; Provide caring and support; Teach "life skills"

The first step is to **increase pro-social bonding** by creating opportunities for students to meet with one another and make friends. Mrs. McCormick does this by:

- Creating a student advisory committee that provides input about reading interests; generates ideas for media-sponsored clubs; identifies topics of interest such as hobbies, sports, and politics that students want to learn about; and formulates a plan to market the school library to peers. Mrs. McCormick enlists the assistance of the business teacher who agrees to help students develop a marketing plan.
- Selecting students to serve on the advisory committee based on desire to participate, not grade point average, popularity, or teacher recommendation. Many students had never been asked to serve on a committee and were thrilled to be considered. She makes the committee meetings special by serving refreshments and inviting the principal to stop by to recognize these students' efforts.
- Encouraging cooperative learning because many students do not respond well to competitive learning situations. Mrs. McCormick assigns students to cooperative work groups based on who they *do not* know so they can broaden their social networks and make new friends. This approach is similar to "Mix It Up," a program that breaks down walls of division that she learned about at tolerance.org, a Web site of the Southern Poverty Law Center to fight hate and promote tolerance.
- Helping students to learn about and develop hobbies and connect with others by creating a monthly after-school program, *HobbyFest*, in which members of the community present information about their hobbies and encourage students to join them. She asks community hobby groups and individuals to donate used books and magazines so students can learn about hobbies.
- Responding to student requests for greater access to the school library by opening up a half-hour early and closing one hour after the school day ends. This new schedule provides time at the end of the school day for clubs to meet in the library and students to work cooperatively on learning assignments and to help each other with homework and to check out books. Mrs. McCormick is applying for grants to establish an after-school program in the school library.
- Writing a column about the school library that has become a regular feature of the monthly newsletter sent to parents.
- Having Open House begin in the library where refreshments are provided, welcoming remarks are presented, and parents can receive a copy of their child's schedule.
- Treating all students warmly and compassionately, addressing them by their first name, and engaging them in conversation about their interests. Mrs. McCormick prides herself on her fair treatment of students, but as she reflects on this she realizes she

is bestowing more attention on popular and academically gifted students. With this realization she becomes more intentional about reaching out to students who are more reserved and not as likely to receive positive attention from teachers. Soon these students are dropping by during the day to say, "Hi!"

The second element is *set clear and consistent boundaries* so students will understand expectations and not be confused by vague and unclear directions. Mrs. McCormick does this by:

- Having student members of the school library committee develop rules of behavior for the library and determine penalties for noncompliance. Mrs. McCormick and the students spend several meetings discussing student behavior in the library and her expectations. She asks committee members to be very specific about how rules should be enforced. She arranges for students to videotape a series of scenarios that showed acceptable and unacceptable library behavior which will be shown during orientation as well as other times. Teachers support this effort by allowing students to earn extra credit.
- Having students draw posters about these rules and post them around the school.

The third element is to *teach life skills* so students are able to navigate their school environment, set goals, and problem solve. Mrs. McCormick does this by:

- Helping students organize clubs and events that require problem-solving, decision-making, and communication skills.
- Having students debate topics of interest. When teachers voice their concerns that students rely too much on Web sites that contain information that is one-sided and prejudicial, Mrs. McCormick decides to change the way she teaches students about Web sites. Rather than beginning these lessons by teaching students how to search and evaluate Web sites, Mrs. McCormick assigns students to groups and gives them topics to search such as "Does day care harm or help children?" She observes as students search for information to answer their topic. After students gather information she has them debate the topic, which helps students learn to express opinions. Often statements made during a debate are countered by the opposing team who question the validity of information used to support an argument or present contradictory information. Only after students recognize the importance of information quality does Mrs. McCormick begin to teach about Web site and database searching and evaluation.
- Teaching life skills through characters in books and information resources.

- Incorporating into lessons life skills that students will need in high school and in the future. Mrs. McCormick discusses life skills whenever a teachable moment occurs and has students practice conflict resolution, stress management, and resistance and assertiveness skills within their cooperative groups. By doing this the school library becomes a laboratory for learning about and practicing life skills.
- Collaborating with the health teacher to support what is being taught in the classroom. Mrs. McCormick talks to other teachers about the importance of life skills and was able to start a "life skill" of the month initiative in which the entire school would stress a particular life skill.
- Showing students how to destress school assignments by planning ahead and not leaving things to the last minute. Mrs. McCormick teaches students various stress management techniques such as confiding in an adult, deep breathing, getting adequate exercise and sleep, and nutritious eating.
- Helping students to realize the importance of believing in effort. Even though many people attribute success to ability, effort, other people, or luck, it is only effort that leads to success (Marzano et al.). When Mrs. McCormick realizes this she makes effort a criterion for successful work and an element on the assignment's rubric.

The fourth element is to ***provide caring and support*** which is giving students respect and encouragement. Henderson and Milstein regard this as the most critical of the six elements that promote resiliency. This is the foundation and basis for the turnaround or holistic school library where students are free to develop and practice life skills in a safe and nonjudgmental environment. Students are not belittled or discussed in a negative connotation. Mrs. McCormick does this by:

- Selecting a media assistant who likes middle school students and can treat them with courtesy and respect. Even though Mrs. McCormick interviews experienced media assistants, she is looking for an individual who is caring, nurturing, and empathetic towards students.
- Engaging students in conversation and being totally present when students are talking to her.
- Listening to students and helping them to problem solve and make decisions. When students make poor decisions that lead to negative results, Mrs. McCormick prompts them to describe what went wrong and to determine better ways to solve the problem.
- Giving students the benefit of the doubt.

The fifth element is to ***set and communicate high expectations*** that leads to quality work. Mrs. McCormick does this by:

- Developing challenging and engaging lessons that require students to be intellectually active and critical thinkers. She bans a type of lesson called "bird units" that require little cognitive engagement from students (Lance and Loertscher). For a "bird unit," students are brought to the library to complete a worksheet about birds (or another topic) and copy and paste information to complete a report. Instead, she collaborates with teachers to develop lesson plans that require students to use information resources to generate and test hypotheses. Using deductive and inductive reasoning to generate and test hypotheses is an effective research-based strategy that increases achievement because students apply knowledge, use information to predict future events, and explain the logic of their thinking which improves communication skills (Marzano, Pickering, and Pollock).
- Collaborating with teachers to develop a joint rubric to assess school library instruction. The rubric covers the content required by state standards, measures the information literacy skills students need to demonstrate, and measures the amount read or the technology used by students (Lance and Loertscher 85). In addition, Mrs. McCormick assesses effort, which is integral to student achievement, through observation and talking with students about their topic.
- Teaching students how to use information and information strategies such as the Big6 and Flip IT! to complete school assignments, as well as to make personal decisions and solve personal problems.

The sixth element is to ***provide opportunities for meaningful participation*** by giving students responsibility for what occurs in the school library and adopting the motto "never do in schools what students can do" (Henderson and Milstein 29). Mrs. McCormick does this by:

- Viewing students as partners who want an effective school library that is meaningful to them. Mrs. McCormick believes that the reason for improved behavior in the school library is because students realize she is a partner in their education and open to their suggestions.
- Encouraging students to volunteer, which helps to increase resiliency and feelings of empathy, which is the ability to care for and understand the feelings of another person (Jones). Mrs. McCormick and the students develop a database of volunteer opportunities in the community which they upload to the school's Web site. This Web site is used extensively by high

school students who must identify places to volunteer to fulfill their community service obligations required for graduation.

Mrs. McCormick believes that her primary role as an educator is to assist youth develop the skills and strengths that enable them to become citizens who can participate in a democratic society. Her secondary role is to develop and manage an effective library program that supports the school's curriculum and student's reading interests and information needs. Without embracing the primary role, it is difficult for the media specialist to fulfill the secondary role. Without accepting the first role, students will not embrace the school library.

A second framework for building resiliency and thereby strengthening youth is the *Library Ladder of Resiliency*, which consists of five rungs, each representing a protective factor found in Werner and Smith's resiliency research. The five rungs are mentoring, reading, problem solving, social skills, and hobbies and interests. Unlike the *Resiliency Wheel*, the *Library Ladder of Resiliency* was developed specifically to encourage librarians to incorporate the findings of the resiliency research into the programs and services of the library. Although the five rungs are likely being carried out, when media specialists realize these are powerful protective factors that build resiliency, they are even more likely to be passionate about mentoring, reading, and encouraging students to develop problem-solving and social skills and hobbies and interests. See Figure 6.3, which is the *Library Ladder of Resiliency*.

Figure 6.3 Library Ladder of Resiliency

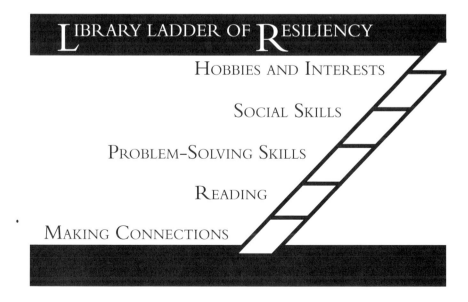

Source: Jami Biles Jones. Reprinted by permission of the author.

The first rung of the *Library Ladder of Resiliency* is mentoring. The purpose of a mentor is to provide guidance, support, reassurance, friendship, and perspective to a young person. Time and again, studies have shown that the most important protective factor for children and teens is caring relationships with adults (Laursen and Birmingham). Media specialists who connect with students in ways that go beyond discipline and maintaining order in the library are more effective instructional partners. They are able to promote literacy by placing the right book at the right time in the hands of students. They are able to bring life to information literacy lessons by teaching these skills using topics meaningful to students. They are able to collaborate with guidance counselors by collecting and disseminating information on mentoring organizations such as Big Brothers/Big Sisters, Boys and Girls Clubs of America, Boys Scouts of America, and Girl Scouts of the USA.

The second protective factor is reading. Werner and Smith (1992) found that many resilient children were competent readers. "Effective reading skills by grade four was one of the most potent predictors of successful adult adaptation" (Krovetz 9). Norman Garmezy's (1983) research on poor black youth in London found that children who exhibited qualities of resilience lived in homes "marked by the presence of books" (75). Media specialists who unite students with books are the heart and soul of effective reading and literacy efforts. This is especially important for middle school students because one developmental task is identity formation. What better way to help a teen establish identity but to experience life through a character who is dealing with similar challenges and issues. Media specialists who understand that reading promotes resiliency are more likely to collaborate with reading specialists to develop book clubs and other reading events.

The third protective factor is problem-solving skills. Sometimes maladaptive children add to their problems because they do not possess the effective problem-solving skills of their more resilient and competent peers (Masten and Coatsworth). Media specialists help students become more resilient by teaching them how to use a model such as ICAN to solve both academic as well as personal problems. ICAN was developed by Dr. Gregory J. Williams of Pacific Lutheran University in Tacoma, Washington.

I   Identify the Problem
C   Can you name some solutions?
A   Analyze the solutions. How will they work?
N   Now, pick one and use it! If it works, great! If not, try again.

The fourth protective factor is social skills. Students who have well-developed social skills are able to make and keep friends. Social skills can be taught by fostering, encouraging, and modeling these behaviors. In Beverly Cleary's *Dear Mr. Henshaw*, sixth-grader Leigh Botts, the new kid in school, is having a difficult time making friends. It is the school janitor who mentors Leigh and advises, "Who wants to be friends with someone who scowls all the time?" Once Leigh understands the importance of smiling, he begins to make friends (80).

School media specialists promote social skills when they support and host activities that encourage students to make friends and work together. An example described previously is Nelle Martin's program, "The Lunch Bunch."

The fifth protective factor is hobbies and interests. Werner and Smith found that "extracurricular activities played an important part in the lives of resilient youth" (57). Hobbies and interests promote competence and self-esteem. Students who face stressful situations and problems may momentarily forget their troubles when they participate in hobbies and interests. Media specialists promote this protective factor when they select and market books and resources that encourage hobbies and interests.

The *Library Ladder of Resiliency* complements the *Resiliency Wheel* and the two can be used together to promote resiliency and improve academic achievement in students. By the end of the school year, Mrs. McCormick notices that students are less apathetic, enter the school library more respectfully, pick up trash, push in their chairs, and exhibit more of the characteristics of students profiled in Figure 6.2 on page 72. Consequently, she is asked to write an article about the impact of the turnaround or holistic library and the process she went through to make these changes, which is the focus of Chapter Seven.

Resources to Learn More about This Topic

Books

Bouncing Back: Dealing with the Stuff Life Throws at You by Jami L. Jones has additional strategies for youth to build their resiliency.

Resiliency in Action: Practical Ideas for Overcoming Risks and Building Strengths in Youth, Families, and Communities, which is edited by Nan Henderson, provides many resources to learn about resiliency. Another useful book is *Schoolwide Approaches for Fostering Resiliency*. These books are available from the Resiliency in Action Web site at <www.resiliency.com>. This organization is a strengths-focused resource to increase self-esteem and resiliency in youth and adults.

Web Sites

For a list of dispositions for librarians, visit the American Library Association's Web site at <www.ala.org/ala/aasl/aaslpubsandjournals/kqweb/kqarchives/volume35/351farmer.htm> and <www.ala.org/ala/yalsa/profdev/yacompetencies/competencies.htm>.

Helping Teens Cope: Ask Dr. Jami at <www.askdrjami.org/index.html> provides resiliency information for teens and educators.

CHAPTER SEVEN

Creating the Holistic Library

It is simple things that strengthen youth. In this book, the tipping point, which is a concept first discussed in the Introduction, is a metaphor that describes how small changes pack a big punch. For the New York City Transit Authority, the tipping point was eradicating graffiti from its trains. The concept of a tipping point works equally well to strengthen youth. The tipping point to create strength and resiliency in youth is mentoring and showing that you care. The tipping point to improve academic achievement is by individualizing instruction. These tipping points focus on the holistic needs of individuals.

Holistic is a term often used in the health realm to describe care that recognizes the interrelatedness of the physical, mental, and spiritual aspects of the individual. Similarly, the concept of holism can be used in librarianship to describe a library that bases services and programs on the physical, mental, and spiritual needs of patrons. The holistic library expands upon traditional services and is proactive in meeting the *whole* needs of the individual. Holistic and turnaround libraries are synonymous. The school library developed by Mrs. McCormick in Chapter Six is holistic because it focuses on the physical needs of students for safety and comfort, their mental or cognitive need to learn and be challenged, and their affective or spiritual need for respect and to connect with others. The holistic school library program is flexible and adjusts to fit the continuing needs of students. Holistic media specialists will like and care about students, hold high expectations for students, are out-of-the-box thinkers, collaborate with teachers to implement strategies that improve academic achievement and strengthen youth, even if it contradicts present philosophy and beliefs of the school.

One framework for developing the holistic library is resiliency because it recognizes that the root of human achievement is nurturing, mentoring, and developing the individual's strengths. An emphasis on instructional strategies is not adequate for many students. The greatest impact occurs when instructional strategies are combined with the protective factors identified in Chapter Six. This interrelatedness between effective education and resiliency is represented in Figure 7.1 on page 82.

Figure 7.1 The Connection Between Effective Education and Resiliency

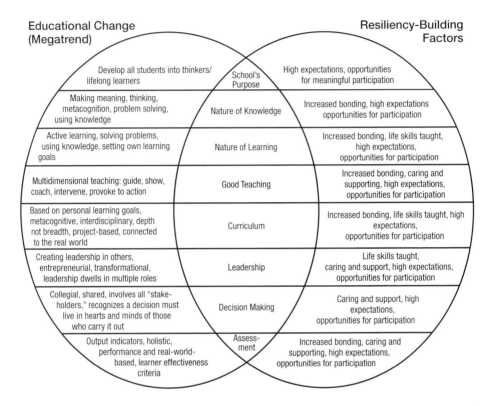

Educational Change (Megatrend) | Resiliency-Building Factors

Educational Change (Megatrend)	School's Purpose	Resiliency-Building Factors
Develop all students into thinkers/ lifelong learners	School's Purpose	High expectations, opportunities for meaningful participation
Making meaning, thinking, metacognition, problem solving, using knowledge	Nature of Knowledge	Increased bonding, high expectations opportunities for participation
Active learning, solving problems, using knowledge, setting own learning goals	Nature of Learning	Increased bonding, life skills taught, high expectations, opportunities for participation
Multidimensional teaching: guide, show, coach, intervene, provoke to action	Good Teaching	Increased bonding, caring and supporting, high expectations, opportunities for participation
Based on personal learning goals, metacognitive, interdisciplinary, depth not breadth, project-based, connected to the real world	Curriculum	Increased bonding, life skills taught, high expectations, opportunities for participation
Creating leadership in others, entrepreneurial, transformational, leadership dwells in multiple roles	Leadership	Life skills taught, caring and support, high expectations, opportunities for participation
Collegial, shared, involves all "stake-holders," recognizes a decision must live in hearts and minds of those who carry it out	Decision Making	Caring and support, high expectations, opportunities for participation
Output indicators, holistic, performance and real-world-based, learner effectiveness criteria	Assessment	Increased bonding, caring and supporting, high expectations, opportunities for participation

Source: Henderson, Nan, and Mike M. Milstein. *Resiliency in Schools: Making It Happen for Students and Educators* p. 8, copyright 2003 by Corwin Press. Reprinted by Permission of Corwin Press Inc.

Schools have tried to alter patterns of failure for students who are at risk for many years without success. This lack of success stems from the fact that school reform usually focuses on changes in operations such as policy and procedures, curriculum, and accountability programs, rather than changes in the social and cultural understandings, beliefs, and biases about the learning needs of children who are economically disadvantaged, of color, have disabilities, and have limited English proficiency. Many researchers have come to the conclusion that deeper issues embedded in the culture of schools might be the cause of academic failure. Chapter Two discussed how many schools continue to operate from a framework of middle class beliefs, assumptions, and expectations that does not create an environment that leads to student success. Unless these deeper issues are addressed, efforts at fundamental change are limited to making small incremental changes that have little meaning.

The Systems Perspective

Fundamental change requires that two things occur. First, it is necessary to correct the assumption that failure is entirely the fault of the child or family's limitations (Wilson). Second, it is necessary to understand that development is a function of a child's ecology. There are many forces that enhance or limit the development of an individual and ways to increase the likelihood of success in the face of forces such as poverty, and other threats to resiliency (Bronfenbrenner; Garbarino). These forces are not unrelated. It helps us to understand "how the individual develops interactively with the immediate social environment" and how the larger social context, such as laws, funding, and historical beliefs affect that immediate environment (Bronfenbrenner 21). In this way we can understand "how the student got this way."

The systems change framework has implications not only for how we think about students, but how we think about our role, opportunities, and efforts to change the school library program, and the school. For example, media specialists whose budgets are severely reduced often lose sight of their dream job as they struggle to maintain basic operations. This outside force changes the way they develop professionally and function in their position—not because the media specialist is inept, but because the pressures from other areas of the system make it difficult for them to do their best.

The ecological perspective of development moves focus away from attributing students' failure to their own or their family's characteristics and challenges the current assumption that poverty is the cause of school failure. The ecological perspective also challenges the media specialist's assumption that funding and other school characteristics prohibit creating a school library program that fosters resiliency. It offers a framework for looking at the culture of schools and how it influences students' success and provides another lens through which we can examine how schools function and respond to at-risk students. By looking beyond the student to identify other factors that foster or hinder children's development and success, we begin to notice that what has been put into place (such as school library policies and rules) either helps or stands in the way of a student's success. The beliefs of school personnel and the organizational constraints of schools create an ecological context for the student that can lead to their failure or make them shine despite conditions such as poverty, race and ethnicity, English language proficiency, or special education status (Zambone et al.; Senge, Fullan). Mrs. McCormick improved academic achievement and strengthened students not by increasing the budget but by connecting to them and providing opportunities for the students to connect to the school library.

The Ecological Systems Change Approach

Media specialists can apply the principles of ecological school system reform to the school library so that it can become an environment in which children thrive, even in a school and district where systems change is not a priority. Longitudinal research indicates that children can become highly resilient when they have just one strong and supportive relationship with an adult and one place where they feel welcome and competent (Sameroff et al.). The research on school and system change indicates several principles that media specialists can adopt in creating an environment and culture that provides all students in the school "somewhere to walk and someone to walk with" as one youth so eloquently gave voice to Sameroff's findings (Jones 495).

Peter Senge, Michael Fullan and other researchers in education reform repeatedly show us that "schools can be recreated, made vital, and substantially renewed not by fiat or command, and not by regulation" but by becoming learning organizations (Senge et al. 5). Research indicates that it is nearly impossible for school professionals to achieve major reforms without strong motivation because real change requires considerable reflection and study—often in areas that make us uncomfortable, such as personal assumptions about poverty and race (Eiseman et al.; Fullan; Villa and Thousand).

Where better than the school library program to create a learning organization that fosters the reflection and is at the heart of motivation to effect real change? When media specialists commit to creating school library programs that promote resiliency for all students and are an integral part of the school, their vision of the kind of library they want to create serves as their motivation to reflect and study, even in areas that may be uncomfortable.

Think About...

What was Mrs. McCormick's motivation for recreating the school library?

The Ecological Systems Change Journey

Media specialists who want to adopt an ecological systems change approach to transform their school or library into a learning organization will need to create a team of collaborators. Collaboration and discussion among the members of the team results in creativity, expertise, and ability that is greater than that of any one individual on the team. This is not a solo journey—inviting others along will not only give needed support but exponentially increase the creativity and intelligence of the media specialist's efforts to change the culture of the library so that it builds students' resiliency and success. Media specialists want to choose collaborators whose knowledge, experience, and perspective are different from their own, as well as individuals with whom they are comfortable. It is also important to choose colleagues who are open to change—the explorers and pioneers at the school. As change occurs and students are increasingly successful, the "wait and see" colleagues are likely to embrace this effort.

Step One

Step one for media specialists is to reflect on their dreams and their role in the school library. Mrs. McCormick began with a reflection on what students in her school needed and how the school library program could respond to those needs.

Can Do...

Revisit Figure 6.2 Profile of a Student Needing Resiliency Improvement on page 72 to see what Mrs. McCormick saw and to guide your own reflection about students in your school and what their needs might be. Shade the figure or make notes about what you think your students might need.

Think About...

What roles do you want your school library to play in the school, particularly on behalf of at-risk students?

Step Two

Step two is to create a vision and mission statement for the school library that succinctly states its purpose. Mrs. McCormick's vision is a school library that is welcoming and helps students to develop skills they will need as they enter high school and beyond. Her vision includes adults who actively engage with students, even if they feel a bit frazzled at the end of the day trying to complete tasks such as shelving after students leave. Her mission is not to have the most complete collection or the neatest space, but to create cooperative learning groups and a library that is an integral part of school and student life. The school library's mission should be based on the mission of the school district as well as the mission of *Information Power*, the national guidelines for school library programs, which is to "ensure that students and staff are effective users of ideas and information" (ALA 101).

To create your vision, revisit Figure 6.3 Profile of a Student with Characteristics of Resiliency on page 77. For each of the six quadrants in the figure, create a picture of how your school library program could make these characteristics possible for an at-risk student. Specifically, answer the following questions:

How can the school library program…

- provide cooperative learning opportunities for students that will enable students to bond with others, help others, and find their voice?
- communicate high expectations and a belief in students' capacities?
- make students feel welcomed and give them a sense of membership and ownership in the school library program?
- motivate and support students to take on new challenges and new learning?
- teach students and give them an opportunity to practice life skills such as problem solving, stress management, conflict resolution, and assertiveness?
- give students a voice in policies and rules and give them positive responsibility to maintain rules?
- provide them with a caring, nurturing connection to caring adults and other students?
- help students see the school library as the *go to* place and through the school library connect them to other programs and activities in the school?

Step Three

Step three is to compare the vision you created for the library in Step one with its reality. The gap between the vision and the reality is what media specialists will want to focus on in their plans for changing the school library. Program evaluation is a tool that, like assessment of students, guides the future of the school library, and documents the efforts and success of media specialists and their programs. Most models and approaches to program evaluation identify two primary, though related, purposes, referred to as formative and summative evaluation. Formative evaluation is ongoing evaluation that is used to guide implementation of a program or effort, while summative evaluation provides a final accounting of a program's effectiveness. In Chapter Six, Mrs. McCormick plans to conduct a summative evaluation at the end of the school year.

While the evaluation literature identifies many more purposes of program evaluation, they essentially fall into one of these two broad categories. Whatever the purpose, the rules of good assessment and research apply. Specifically, the questions the evaluation intends to answer are meaningful and clearly identified; the methods used and the data collected to answer those questions are real and trustworthy; and the results are analyzed and reported in a way that is useful to the media specialist and other stakeholders in the school library.

Media specialists with a clear vision and mission statement, well-developed goals, partnerships that push their thinking and help them learn, and a solid plan for reaching those goals have an excellent foundation for a program evaluation process that will ensure effective implementation of that plan. You evaluate whether you are achieving your goals by collecting information that makes sense. For example, if one goal is to create a climate of welcome for all students, you could survey students and teachers or observe usage of the school library and length of visit before and after changes have been made.

There are numerous models and approaches to program evaluation. How elaborate and formal an evaluation method media specialists might use will depend on their resources and expectations. The essence of program evaluation is to be willing to learn about the needs and expectations of the persons whom the media specialist wants to reach through the school library program and be open to understanding how well the program is working.

The data the media specialist collects may be quantitative, such as keeping track of the number of books circulated or number of students who visited the library; or qualitative, such as conducting a focus group with students to learn their perceptions and opinions about what makes them feel welcome in the library; or a combination of both. The data the media specialist chooses to gather is determined both by the evaluation questions and by the resources the media specialist has available. Whatever the process, it is important to set up a timeline and procedures for reviewing that data and using it to reinforce or make changes in the program plan and its implementation. Carter McNamara, on the Web site <www.managementhelp. org/evaluatn/ fnleval.htm> provides a guide to program evaluation and identifies numerous evaluation resources. He also makes the point that media specialists do not need to be experts to implement a useful program evaluation.

Craig Noonan and Nan Henderson in the book *Resiliency in Action: Practical Ideas for Overcoming Risks and Building Strengths in Youth, Families, and Communities* identify the following steps to conducting a program evaluation (52-56):

1. *Identify questions and involve others*: Work with colleagues who are part of your systems change effort to identify questions that are important to answer—first about the current school library program and how it compares to your vision. Second you will identify new questions that will help you and your colleagues determine whether your plans for change are working.
2. *Prioritize questions*: Identify the questions that are most important for you and your colleagues to help with planning for and implementing effective systems change.
3. *Define the questions*: In this very important step, clarify questions so you can answer them in measurable ways. For example, a question such as "Do students come to the school library and spend more time here meaningfully engaged?" can be refined to "How much time do students a) spend in the school library during the week; and b) engage in cooperative learning activities while there?"
4. *Choose the measurement tools*: Identify how you will get answers to your questions. First consider what is already in place, such as a sign-in sheet that logs how much time a student is in the library at one time. Second, look for measurement tools that will give you answers you can trust and quantify. According to Noonan and Henderson, "most variables . . . in program evaluation fall into one of the following categories: attitudes, knowledge, skills, behavior, or environmental factors. This data can be collected by self-reports, interviews, surveys, and records in archival sources, observations and/or current records" (54).
5. *Design your evaluation*: This is simply a description of how you will collect your data.
6. *Implement your plan*: First try out your measurements and see if they will answer your questions and if they are doable. Once you have

refined the plan, implement it—and you are on the way to gathering the data needed to determine the kinds of changes you might want to make to realize your vision!

7. *Organize and analyze your data*: This is an important part of any plan. For example, you may review sign-in sheets weekly and tally the number of students and time spent in the library over a period of one month.

8. *Share the results*: Compile your results and share them with your colleagues in a report that includes the questions, methods for evaluating, methods for analysis of data, and the results. This will help guide the systems change plan as well as the next phase of evaluation.

9. *Start all over again with new questions*: Once changes have been made, you will want to evaluate whether the plan is working. At each phase of your systems change and your school library program's operation you will always have new questions to answer about what is working well and what needs to be improved.

Step Four

Once media specialists have a clear picture of what they want to accomplish for their school library, they will bring together a group of colleagues to get their input and buy-in. The media specialist will share his vision and the results of his evaluation with the group at this point. This collaboration creates the *collective expertise* on how to build students' and adults' resiliency both through pooling their knowledge and experience, and learning new things together, such as what Mrs. McCormick did through reading *Resiliency in Schools: Making it Happen for Students and Educators* by Nan Henderson and Mike Milstein.

Can Do...

Identify at least four colleagues that you will ask to help create a shared vision.

Together, the team reflects on the attitudes and perceptions that can further or interfere with making the changes necessary to bring this shared vision to fruition. Taking time to reflect on assumptions and beliefs about students, schools, and their own roles enables media specialists and other school personnel to see how these attitudes and assumptions could limit their vision of a school library that benefits all students. Creating a safe place for team members to explore each individual's assumptions and beliefs about culture, race, class, poverty, equity, and achievement is an important step that can lead them to empowering theories about learning and teaching.

Mrs. McCormick might want to find a colleague who uses cooperative learning strategies in her classroom, a colleague who has expertise in literacy and remediation, an administrator who would like to increase the school's connection with families and the community, and perhaps a school counselor who is concerned about students' life skills. Together they can each share their knowledge and skills, further study resiliency and ways to create the kind of welcoming, nurturing atmosphere she envisions for students, and refine her vision.

Study the ways in which the school library is interdependent with the school and community. Like a stone tossed into a pond, every change, no matter how small, ripples throughout the school. This can result in barriers or *push back* from others in the school, making it difficult to achieve the desired change.

Think About...

What are some of the group member's assumptions and beliefs about students as they relate to the school library? What are some of your frustrations with students? How might these frustrations represent your assumptions, preferences, or style, rather than real problems from the students?

Step Five

Create a plan for realizing the vision and mission for the school library.

Can Do...

Identify three new things the group would like to learn more about as they begin to put together their plan.

Step Six

From this study, identify the tipping point—the first small change that will bring about great change. This is where our analogy comes to life: It is much like a small tug boat turns a large ship once it finds the right point along the hull to begin pushing.

As Fullan said, "change is ubiquitous and relentless (vii). Understanding systems change and ensuring that the school library, if not the whole school, is a learning organization makes it possible to engage in change proactively and productively, rather than being swept by the forces of change into practices, conditions, and outcomes that do not lead to a school library that benefits all students. Together, the media specialist and team study their vision, assumptions, and the systemic nature of the school in which they work. They also seek to learn any new knowledge or skills they may require to realize their dream.

In this chapter we've described a systems change process that may seem cumbersome, but will get results for the school library program and for the students, which will reverberate throughout the school. We believe that the school library program and the media specialist are central to the school community and its mission to educate children. We also believe that the school library program is the part of the school that touches all students and staff, supports all programs and instruction, and provides access to information and the world of knowledge and resources beyond the school's walls. Consequently, the school library program should be the heart of the school and the place where students are most likely to develop the resiliency they need to be successful. As such, it is critical to take the time to create an environment and program that cultivates the type of students described in Figure 6.2 Profile of a Student with Characteristics of Resiliency on page 72.

As the early chapters in this book have made clear, we are losing too many students and the consequences for them and for our society are tremendous. Many of the effective approaches and strategies discussed throughout the book do not require a lot of fiscal resources, but they do require heart, commitment, and creativity. If you are reading this last chapter, your commitment and heart are already evident. We hope that we have given information that will spark your creativity as well. If you go back to Figure 7.1 The Connection Between Effective Education and Resiliency on page 82, you will see that the changes identified in the left circle fit well with the nature of the school library program and the expertise of media specialists. The school library program is uniquely suited for inspiring students to be lifelong learners, engaging them in active learning that is interdisciplinary, and connecting learning and curriculum to personal goals, problem solving, and using and building up knowledge and experiences.

As you embark on changing your system, remember that an important aspect is to build coalitions with colleagues; to actively pursue, with them, new knowledge and skills; and to start small but thoughtfully. We have included numerous resources and exercises throughout the book to help you learn and achieve your goals for your school library program. Everything you do will have a positive effect on the school. No matter how challenging the school environment may seem, the school library program can achieve the most important feature of building resiliency—creating nurturing relationships and welcoming environments for students. You can anticipate that the impact of this change on the students and the climate of the school will be like the way a smile on one person's face can change the atmosphere of a meeting or a group. Most notably, engaging in a systems change process that relies on building collaborative relationships and creating learning communities will build your resiliency and that of your colleagues.

Resources to Learn More about This Topic

Books

Benard, Bonnie. *Resiliency: What We Have Learned*. San Francisco: WestEd, 2004.

Krovetz, Martin L. *Fostering Resiliency: Expecting All Students to Use Their Minds and Hearts Well*. Thousand Oaks: Corwin Press, Inc., 1999.

Thomsen, Kate. *Building Resilient Students: Integrating Resiliency into What You Already Know and Do*. Thousand Oaks: Corwin Press, Inc., 2002.

Web Sites

Tucson Resiliency Initiative at <www.tucsonresiliency> is a grassroots effort to promote resiliency that was formed in 1998. Ideas for providing caring and support are located at <www.tucsonresiliency.org/ideas.cfm>.

Visit <www.ala.org/ala/aasl/aaslproftools/positionstatements/aasl positionstatementrole.cfm> to read the American Association of School Librarian's (AASL) *Position Statement on the Role of the School Library Media Program.*

The Basic Guide to Program Evaluation is available at <www. managementhelp.org/evaluatn/fnl_eval.htm#anchor1575679>.

Resources for conducting program evaluation are available on the Web site of the American Association of School Librarians at <www.ala.org/ala/aasl/aaslproftools/resourceguides/evaluation.cfm>.

WORKS CITED

Section One

Introduction

Benard, Bonnie. "How to be a Turnaround Teacher/Mentor." <www.resiliency. com/htm/turnaround.htm>.

Gladwell, Malcolm. *The Tipping Point: How Little Things Can Make a Big Difference*. New York: Little, Brown and Company, 2000.

Thernstrom, Abigail, and Stephan Thernstrom. *No Excuses: Closing the Racial Gap in Learning*. New York: Simon & Schuster, 2003.

Chapter One

"America's Silent Epidemic." *Oprah*. ABC. WCTI, New Bern, NC: 11-12 Apr. 2006.

Balfanz, Robert, and Nettie Legters. "Locating the Dropout Crisis: Which High Schools Produce the Nation's Dropouts? Where Are They Located? Who Attends Them?" Sep. 2004. 20 Apr. 2006 <www.csos.jhu.edu/tdhs/rsch/ Locating_Dropouts.pdf>.

Cushman, Kathleen. "Help Us Care Enough to Learn." *Educational Leadership* 63.5 (2006): 34-37.

Greene, Jay P., and Greg Forster. "Public High School Graduation and College Readiness Rates in the United States." Sep. 2003. Manhattan Institute for Research. 20 Apr. 2006 <www.manhattan-institute.org/html/ewp_ 03.htm>.

Hall, Daria. "Getting Honest about Grad Rates: How States Play the Numbers and Students Lose." June 2005. The Education Trust. 15 Apr. 2007 <www. edtrust.org>.

Kozol, Jonathan. *The Shame of the Nation: The Restoration of Apartheid Schooling in America*. New York: Crown Publishers, 2005.

Riggs, Jacki Pieracci, Garrey E. Carruthers, and Beata I. Thorstensen. "If You Build It They Will Come: Investing in Public Education." 19 Apr. 2006 <abec.unm.edu/resources/gallery/present/invest_in_ed.pdf>.

Schargel, Franklin P. "Helping Students Graduate: Tools and Strategies to Prevent School Dropouts." 18th Annual At-Risk National Youth Forum. Myrtle Beach, S.C. 17 Feb. 2006.

Swanson, Christopher B. "Who Graduates? Who Doesn't? A Statistical Portrait of Public High School Graduation, Class of 2001." 2003. The Urban Institute. 19 Apr. 2006 <www.urban.org/UploadedPDF/410934_WhoGraduates.pdf>.

Wimberly, George L., and Richard J. Noeth. "College Readiness Begins in Middle School." ACT. 20 Apr. 2006 <www.act.org/path/policy/pdf/CollegeReadiness.pdf>.

Chapter Two

Almeida, Cheryl, Cassius Johnson, and Adria Steinbert. "Making Good on a Promise: What Policymakers Can Do to Support the Educational Persistence of Drop Outs." *Jobs for the Future.* 20 Apr. 2006 <www.jff.org/~jff/Documents/MkingGood_Sum.pdf>.

Astuto, Terry, David Clark, and Anne-Marie Read. *Roots of Reform: Challenging the Assumptions That Control Educational Reform.* Bloomington: Phi Delta Kappa Educational Foundation, 1994.

Boykin, A. Wade. "Talent Development, Cultural Deep Structure, and School Reform: Implications for African Immersion Initiatives." *Improving Schools for African American Students: A Reader for Educational Leaders*. Eds. Sheryl Denbo and Lynson Moore Beaulieu. Springfield: Charles C. Thomas, 2002.

Capps, Randolph, Michael Fix, Julie Murray, Jason Ost, Jeffrey Passel, and Shinta Herwantoro. *The New Demography of America's Schools: Immigration and the No Child Left Behind Act.* The Urban Institute. 1 June 2007 <www.urban.org/UploadedPDF/311230_new_demography.pdf>.

Cummins, Jim. "Empowering Minority Students: A Framework for Intervention." *Harvard Educational Review* 56.1 (1986): 18-36.

Frey, William, and Richard DeVol. "America's Demography in the New Century: Aging Baby Boomers and New Immigrants as Major Players." 8 Mar. 2000. *Milken Institute Policy Brief* 9. 20 May 2007 <www.urban.org/UploadedPDF/311230_new_demography.pdf>.

Gould, William T. S., and Allan M. Findlay. *Population and the Changing World Order.* New York: Wiley, 1994.

Kozol, Jonathan. *The Shame of the Nation: The Restoration of Apartheid Schooling in America.* New York: Crown Publishers, 2005.

Orfield, Gary, Daniel Losen, Jennifer Wald, and Christopher Swanson. "Losing Our Future: How Minority Youth Are Being Left Behind by the Graduation Rate Crisis." *The Urban Institute*. 6 Apr. 2006 <www.urban.org/url.cfm?ID=410936>.

Payne, Ruby K. *A Framework for Understanding Poverty*. Highlands: Aha! Process, 2005.

Perry, Bruce. "Stress, Trauma, and Post-Traumatic Stress Disorders in Children: An Introduction." *Childhood Trauma Interdisciplinary Education Series*. 1999. 1 Apr. 2006 <www.ChildTrauma.org>.

Phillips, Meredith, James Crouse, and John Ralph. "Does the Black-White Test Gap Widen After Children Enter School?" *The Black-White Test Score Gap*. Eds. Christopher Jencks and Meredith Phillips. Washington, D.C.: Brookings Institution Press, 1998.

Pong, Suet-ling. "Immigrant Children's School Performance." *Population Research Institute*. The Pennsylvania State University. 2003. 3 Sept. 2006 <athens.pop.psu.edu/allen/WpByAuth.cfm?AuthorID=661>.

Short, Deborah, and Jane Echevarria. "Teacher Skills to Support English Language Learners." *Educational Leadership* 62:4 (2004): 8-13.

Smith, Deborah Deutsch. *An Introduction to Special Education: Teaching in an Age of Opportunity*. 5th ed. Boston: Prentice-Hall, 2006.

Spring, Joel. *Deculturalization and the Struggle for Equality: A Brief History of the Education of Dominated Cultures in the United States*. 4th ed. Boston: McGraw-Hill, 2004.

Taylor, Lorraine, and Catherine Whittaker. *Bridging Multiple Worlds: Case Studies of Diverse Educational Communities*. Boston: Allyn & Bacon, 2003.

Thompson, Gail L. *Through Ebony Eyes: What Teachers Need to Know But are Afraid to Ask About African American Students*. San Francisco: Jossey-Bass, 2004.

Velasquez, Patrick. *The Relationship Between Cultural Development, Sense of Belonging, and Persistence Among Chicanos in Higher Education: An Exploratory Study*. Nov. 1999. 1 Oct. 2006 <eric.ed.gov/ERICDocs/data/ericdocs2/content_storage_01/0000000b/80/10/a4/82.pdf>.

Williams, Belinda, ed. "The Nature of the Achievement Gap: The Call for a Vision to Guide Change." *Closing the Achievement Gap: A Vision for Changing Beliefs and Practices*. 3rd ed. Alexandria: Association for Supervision and Curriculum Development, 2003.

Zambone, Alana, Carol Howard, and Kimberly Elliott. *The ABLE Guidebook: Achieving Better Learning Through Equity*. Newton: Education Development Center, 2002.

Chapter Three

Drew, Sam. "The Power of School-Community Collaboration in Dropout Prevention." *Helping Students Graduate: A Strategic Approach to Dropout Prevention*. Eds. Jay Smink and Franklin Schargel. Larchmont: Eye on Education, 2004.

Duttweiler, Patricia. "Systemic Renewal: What Works?" *Helping Students Graduate: A Strategic Approach to Dropout Prevention*. Eds. Jay Smink and Franklin Schargel. Larchmont: Eye on Education, 2004.

Yell, Michael, and Erik Drasgow. *No Child Left Behind: A Guide for Professionals*. Upper Saddle River: Pearson Prentice Hall, 2005.

Section Two

Chapter Four

Lance, Keith Curry. "Impact of School Library Media Programs on Academic Achievement." *Teacher Librarian* 29.3 (2002): 29-34.

Lance, Keith Curry. "Proof of the Power: Recent Research on the Impact of School Library Media Programs on the Academic Achievement of U.S. Public School Students." *ERIC Clearinghouse on Information and Technology.* 2000. 15 Feb. 2007 <www.ericdigests.org/2002-2/proof.htm>.

Lance, Keith Curry, and David Loertscher. *Powering Achievement: School Library Media Programs Make a Difference: The Evidence.* 3rd ed. Salt Lake City: Hi Willow Research & Publishing, 2005.

Lance, Keith Curry, Lynda Welborn, and Christine Hamilton-Pennell. *The Impact of School Library Media Centers on Academic Achievement.* Castle Rock: Hi Willow Research and Publishing, 1993.

Lonsdale, Michele. "Impact of School Libraries on Student Achievement: A Review of the Research." Australian Council for Educational Research. 2003. 20 Feb. 2007 <www.asla.org.au/research/index.htm>.

Smalley, Topsy N. "College Success: High School Librarians Make the Difference." *The Journal of Academic Librarianship* 30.3 (2004): 193-198.

Todd, Ross. *A Summary of the Ohio Research Study: Student Learning through Ohio School Libraries.* Ohio Educational Library Media Association. 15 Dec. 2003. 28 Feb. 2007 <www.oelma.org/StudentLearning/documents/OELMAResearchStudy8page.pdf>.

Whelan, Debra Lau. "13,000 Kids Can't Be Wrong: A New Ohio Study Shows How School Libraries Help Students Learn." *School Library Journal* Feb. 2004: 46-50.

Chapter Five

Benard, Bonnie. "Fostering Resiliency in Kids." *Educational Leadership* 51.3 (1993): 44-8.

Duke, Nell K. "For the Rich It's Richer: Print Experiences and Environments Offered to Children in Very Low- and Very High-Socioeconomic Status First-Grade Classrooms." *American Educational Research Journal* 37.2 (2000): 441-478.

Edwards, Clifford H. "Moral Classroom Communities for Student Resiliency." *The Education Digest* 67.2 (2001): 15-20.

Haggerty, Robert J., Lonnie R. Sherrod, Norman Garmezy, and Michael Rutter. *Stress, Risk, and Resilience in Children and Adolescents: Processes, Mechanisms, and Interventions.* Cambridge: Cambridge University Press, 1996.

Henderson, Nan. E-mail interview. 10 Oct. 2006.

Henderson, Nan, ed. *Resiliency in Action: Practical Ideas for Overcoming Risks and Building Strengths in Youth, Families, & Communities.* Ojai: Resiliency in Action, 2007.

Marzano, Robert J. *What Works in Schools: Translating Research into Action.* Alexandria: Association for Supervision and Curriculum Development, 2003.

National Dropout Prevention Network/Center. 15 Feb. 2007 <www.dropoutprevention.org>.

Werner, Emmy E., and Ruth S. Smith. *Journeys from Childhood to Midlife: Risk, Resilience, and Recovery.* Ithaca: Cornell University Press, 2001.

Werner, Emmy E., and Ruth S. Smith. *Overcoming the Odds: High Risk Children from Birth to Adulthood.* Ithaca: Cornell University Press, 1992.

Section Three

Introduction

The Association for Supervision and Curriculum Development. "The Learning Compact Redefined: A Call to Action." 2007. 4 June 2007 <www.ascd.org/learningcompact>.

Dispositions

Bradburn, Frances, and Jason W. Osborne. "Shared Leadership Makes an IMPACT in North Carolina." 20 May 2007 <www.eschoolnews.com/news/ShowStory.cfm?ArticleID=6916>.

"Dispositions of Candidates from Our Own Assessments." University of Arkansas at Little Rock College of Education. 20 May 2007 <www.ncate.org/documents/IOFall05/Dispositions_of_Candidates.ppt#5>.

Kouzes, James, M., and Barry Z. Posner. *Leadership Challenge.* 3rd ed. San Francisco: Jossey-Bass, 2002.

Whaley, David C. "Assessing the Disposition of Teacher Education Candidates." 20 Feb. 2007 <www.nesinc.com/PDFs/1999_11Whaley.pdf>.

Chapter Six

Henderson, Nan, and Mike M. Milstein. *Resiliency in Schools: Making it Happen for Students and Educators.* Thousand Oaks: Corwin Press, 2003.

Jones, Jami L. *Bouncing Back: Dealing with the Stuff Life Throws at You.* New York: Franklin Watts, 2007.

Krovetz, Martin L. *Fostering Resiliency: Expecting All Students to Use Their Hearts and Minds Well.* Thousand Oaks: Corwin, 1999.

Lance, Keith Curry, and David V. Loertscher. "No More Bird Units: A Five-Minute Discussion Starter for School Library Media Specialists and Teachers." *Powering Achievement: School Library Media Programs Make a Difference: The Evidence*. 3rd ed. Salt Lake City: Hi Willow Research & Publishing, 2005.

Laursen, Erik K., and Scott M. Birmingham. "Caring Relationships as a Protective Factor for *At-Risk* Youth: An Ethnographic Study." *Families in Society: The Journal of Contemporary Human Services* 84 (2005): 240-246.

Marzano, Robert J. "Direct Vocabulary Instruction: An Idea Whose Time Has Come." *Closing the Achievement Gap*. Ed. Belinda Williams. 2nd ed. Alexandria: Association for Supervision and Curriculum Development, 2003.

Marzano, Robert J., Debra J. Pickering, and Jane E. Pollock. *Classroom Instruction that Works: Research-Based Strategies for Increasing Student Achievement*. Alexandria: Association for Supervision and Curriculum Development, 2001.

Masten, Ann S., and Douglas J. Coatsworth. "The Development of Competence in Favorable and Unfavorable Environments: Lessons from Research on Successful Children." *American Psychologist* Feb. 1998: 205-220.

Werner, Emmy E., and Ruth S. Smith. *Overcoming the Odds: High Risk Children from Birth to Adulthood*. Ithaca: Cornell University Press, 1992.

Chapter Seven

Benard, Bonnie. "Fostering Resiliency in Kids." *Educational Leadership* 51.3 (1993): 41, 44-48.

Bronfenbrenner, Urie. *The Ecology of Human Development: Experiments By Nature and Design*. Cambridge: Harvard University Press, 1979.

Cuban, Larry. "Myths about Changing Schools and the Case of Special Education." *Remedial and Special Education* 17.2 (1996): 75-92.

Eisman, Jeffrey, Douglas Fleming, and Diane Roodi. *The school improvement leaders: Four perspectives on change in schools*. Andover: The Regional Laboratory, 1990.

Fullan, Michael. *Change Forces: Probing the Depths of Educational Reform*. Levitt Town: The Falmer Press, 1998.

Gabarino, James. *Children and families in the social environment*. New York: Aldine Transactions, 1992.

Henderson, Nan, and Mike M. Milstein. *Resiliency in Schools: Making It Happen for Students and Educators*. Thousand Oaks: Corwin Press, 2003.

Jones, Jami L. "Somewhere to Walk and Someone to Walk With": Resiliency Experts Discuss How Libraries and Librarians Strengthen Youth. *Voice of Youth Advocates* 29.2 (2007): 495-498.

Masten, Ann S. "Ordinary Magic: Resilience Process in Development." *American Psychologist* March 2001: 227-238.

Noonan, C., and Nan Henderson. "An Introduction to Program Evaluation: A Step-By-Step Guide to Getting Started." *Resiliency in Action: Practical Ideas for Overcoming Risks and Building Strengths in Youth, Families, and Communities.* Ed. Nan Henderson. Ojai: Resiliency in Action, 2007.

Sameroff, Arnold. "Environmental Risk Factors in Infancy." *Pediatrics* 102.5 (1998): 1287-1292.

Senge, Peter, Nelda Cambron-McCabe, Timothy Lucas, Bryan Smith, Janis Dutton, and Art Kleiner. *Schools that Learn: A Fifth Discipline Fieldbook for Educators, Parents, and Everyone Who Cares about Education.* New York: Doubleday, 2000.

Villa, Richard, and Jaqueline Thouand. *Restructuring public school systems: Strategies for organizational change and progress.* In Richard Villa, Jaqueline Thousand, and Susan Stainback. *Restructuring for caring and effective education: An administrative guide to creating inclusive schools.* Baltimore: Paul H. Brookes, 1993.

Werner, Emmy E., and Ruth S. Smith. *Overcoming the Odds: High Risk Children for Birth to Adulthood.* Ithaca: Cornell University Press, 1992.

Wilson, William Julius. "The Role of the Environment in the Black-White Test Score Gap." *The Black-White Test Score Gap.* Eds. Christopher Jencks and Meredith Phillips. Washington, D.C.: Brookings Institution Press, 1998.

Zambone, Alana, Carol Howard, and Kimberly Elliott. *The ABLE Guidebook: Achieving Better Learning through Equity.* Newton: Education Development Center, 2002.

INDEX

A

A Nation at Risk, 24, 25, 30
Accountability, 25, 26, 30, 82
ACT
  College Readiness Begins in Middle School,
  8, 94
Active learning, 58, 91
Additive pedagogy, 13
African-American
  after-school opportunities, 58
  high school graduation, 7, 13
  population statistics, 12, 18
  race and ethnicity, 12, 13, 15
  reading, 13, 38
  special education 18
Alliance for Excellent Education, 4
Almeida, Cheryl, 10, 94
America 2000, 25
American Indian
  high school graduation rate, 8
  population statistics, 12
  race and ethnicity, 12
  special education, 18
American Library Association, 30, 64, 79
American workplace, 3
Americans with Disabilities Act (ADA), 29-30
America's Silent Epidemic, 6, 93
*An Essential Connection: How Quality School
  Library Media Programs Improve Student
  Achievement*, 44
Asians
  high school graduation rate, 5, 8
  population statistics, 12
  race and ethnicity, 12
Astuto, Terry, 9, 94
At-risk students. See also high risk
  characteristics, 18
  education, 9, 21, 23, 57, 83
  laws, 24
Attention Deficit Disorder/Attention-Deficit
  Hyperactivity Disorder (ADD/ADHD),
  18-24

B

Balfanz, Robert, 5, 93
Baughman, James C., x
Baumbach, Donna, x
Behavior/emotional disorders (BED)
  in media center, 74-76
  special education, 18, 19, 28
Benard, Bonnie, 1, 46, 50, 60
Bilingual education, 16-17
Bill & Melinda Gates Foundation, 8
Boykin, A. Wade, 13
Bracy, Pauletta Brown, 44
Brehm, Katherine, 60
Broken windows theory, x
Burgin, Robert J., 44

C

Callison, Daniel, x
Can Do…, 5, 13, 14, 17, 26, 28, 29, 37, 53, 54,
  59, 85, 87, 89, 90
Capps, Randolph, 14-15, 94
Caucasians
  high school graduation rate, 8
  population statistics, 15
  special education, 18
Change agents, ix
Change models. See systems change
Chomsky, Noam, 68
College readiness, 7-8
Colorado Study, 35-36
Colorado State Library, 44
Constructivist, 13
Cooperative learning, 60, 72-73, 85, 88, 90
Cumulative Promotion Index (CPI), 5, 10, 13
Curriculum, 13, 16, 19, 36-37, 39, 40-41, 44,
  51, 53, 77, 82, 91
Cushman, Kathleen, 6

Persons of color, 12
Phillips, Meredith, 12-13, 95, 99
Pickering, D.J., 76, 98
Pollock, J.E. 76, 98
Pong, Suet-ling, 15, 95
Poverty
  characteristics, 6, 10, 24, 29, 45-46, 89
  definition, 11
  education, 57
  generational, 11
  impact on students, 12, 47, 83-84
  library, 67
  situational, 11
Problem-solving skills. See also resiliency
  Library Ladder of Resiliency, 77-78
Professional development, 58
Program evaluation, 86-88, 92, 99
Promoting Power Index (PPI), 5, 10, 13
Protective factors. See also resiliency
  definition, 46
  developing, 49, 70-71, 81
  environmental, 1
  media specialists, 48, 77
  research, 47-48
*Public High School Graduation and College
  Readiness*, 7, 93

—
R

Race and ethnicity, 4, 10, 12-15, 83
Ralph, John, 95
Reading, Library Ladder of Resiliency, 78
Riggs, Jacki Pieracci, 4, 93
Resiliency, xi, 1, 9, 20, 29, 33, 45-50, 67, 70.
  See also Kauai Longitudinal Study. See also
  Smith, Ruth. See also Werner, Emmy E.
Resiliency in Action, 46-48, 60, 79, 88, 97, 99
Resiliency Wheel, 68, 71. See also
  Henderson, Nan
Rodney, Marcia, 34, 36, 44
Rutter, Michael, 46, 96

—
S

Sameroff, Arnold, 84, 99
Schargel, Frank, 3-4, 57, 93, 95
Section 504 of the *Vocational Rehabilitation
  Act* of 1973, 27-30
Senge, Peter, 83
Service learning, 58
Sherrod Lonnie R., 96
Short, Deborah, 16, 21, 95

Situational poverty, 11. See also Payne, Ruby.
Smalley, Topsy N., 38
Smink, Jay, 57, 95
Smith, Bryan, 99
Smith, Deborah Deutsch, 14, 95
Smith, Ruth, 33, 46-48, 67, 77-79, 97-99. See
  also Werner, Emmy E.
Social skills, Library Ladder of Resiliency, 78
Socioeconomic status (SES)
  effect on education, 10, 37
  hispanics, 15
  immigrant, 15
  library, 37
  low-, 1, 10-12, 54, 96
Southern Poverty Law Center, 73
Special education. See also Attention deficit
  disorder/attention deficit hyperactivity
  disorder; behavior/emotional disorders
  benefits, 19
  eligibility for services, 17-19, 27-28
  Gifted, 18
  high school graduation rate, 18
  individualized education plan (IEP), 59
  impact, 10
  laws, 27, 29-30
  media center, 20, 28, 29
  race and ethnicity, 18
  trauma, 19
Spring, Joel, 95
standup.org Web site, 5, 8
Steinbert, Adria, 94
Student achievements, factors that influence,
  50-61. See also Marzano, Robert J.
Swanson, Christopher, v, 5, 94
Sykes, Judith Anne, 60
Systemic renewal, 56, 95
Systems change model, 83

—
T

Taylor, Lorraine, 14, 95
Tennessee, 6
Thernstrom, Abigail and Steven, ix, 93
"Think Abouts," 7, 9-10, 12, 15, 19-20, 29, 30,
  49, 52, 68, 70, 84-85, 87, 90
Thomsen, Kate, 92
Thompson, Gail, 13, 95
Thousand, Jacqueline, 99
Title IV: Safe and Drug-Free Schools and
  Communities Act, 24, 26, 50
Tipping point, x, xi, 81, 90
*The Tipping Point: How Little Things Can
  Make a Big Difference*, x, 93

Todd, Ross, x, 38, 96
Traditional bilingual education, 17. See also
   English language classroom.

U

U.S. Census Bureau statistics, 12
U.S. Department of Education, 4, 12, 24, 26,
   37
Urban Institute, 4-5, 8, 94

V

Velasquez, Patrick, 14, 95
Villa, Richard, 84, 99
Vocabulary development, 55, 67-68

W

Wald, Jennifer, 94
Welborn, Lynda, 34
Werner, Emmy E., 33, 46-48, 67, 77-78, 97-99
Whaley, David C., 64, 97
Whalan, Debra Lau, 38, 96
Wimberly, George L., 8, 94
Williams, Belinda, 12, 95, 98
Williams, Gregory J., 78. See also ICAN
Wilson, Williams Julius, 83, 99
Wise, Bob, 4
"Withitness," 53
Whittaker, Catherine, 14, 95

Y

Yell, Michael, 24-26, 95

Z

Zambone, Alana, 14, 83, 95, 99
Zucker, Steven, 60

ABOUT THE AUTHORS

Jami L. Jones

Jami L. Jones is an Assistant Professor in the Department of Library Science and Instructional Technology at East Carolina University in Greenville, North Carolina. The author has worked in schools in Florida, North Carolina, and Delaware as a media specialist, directed public libraries, and worked in state libraries. In 2002, Dr. Jones became a member of the first cohort of media specialists to achieve National Board Certification. Dr. Jones is the creator of the Florida Association of Media in Education's Amanda Award that recognizes media specialists who develop programs that promote teen resiliency and self-esteem. She is the author of *Bouncing Back: Dealing with the Stuff Life Throws at You* (Franklin Watts, 2007) and *Helping Teens Cope: Resources for School Library Media Specialists and Other Youth Workers* (Linworth, 2003).

Dr. Jones received a BA in Sociology from Mills College, an MLS from the University of Maryland, and a Ph.D. in Information Science from Nova Southeastern University. The author can be contacted at jonesj@ecu.edu or her Web site at <www.askdrjami.org>.

Alana M. Zambone

Alana M. Zambone is an Assistant Professor in the Department of Curriculum and Instruction at East Carolina University in Greenville, North Carolina. During her 30-year career, the author has taught children and youth with special needs, pre-service teachers and other professionals. Dr. Zambone provided consultation and technical assistance to effect school change and develop formal and informal education programs across the United States and in the Asia/Pacific and Latin America regions. Dr. Zambone directed development of the National Board Certification for Professional Teaching Standards Assessment for Teachers of Students with Exceptional Needs for Educational Development Center, Inc. and was a founder and Senior Research Fellow for the Institute for Equity in Schools addressing issues of equity and school change for at-risk students.

Dr. Zambone received her BA in elementary and special education from the University of North Carolina at Chapel Hill; MS in Human Development Liaison from George Peabody College for Teachers, and her Ph.D. in special education from Vanderbilt University. The author can be contacted at zambonea@ecu.edu.